Hmmm...Food For Thought

A YEAR OF DEVOTION AND SUSTENANCE

Michael U. Anthony

ISBN: 0692856587

ISBN 13: 9780692856581

Library of Congress Control Number: 2017903418

Michael U. Anthony, St. Thomas, Virgin Islands

Contents

All scripture is presented in the *King James Version* as found on https://www.Biblegateway.com

Author's Note

Thank you for dedicating time to make this collection of devotional thoughts part of your day. This is not an attempt by me to give you an earth-shattering experience! Rather, I give you a few points for reflection, as the presentations are considered in light of your relationship (or lack thereof) with the Lord Jesus Christ.

The thoughts expounded here are from the ten-year collection of my radio broadcasts and moments of inspiration. Each reading is best studied with your Bible close at hand, and digested and pondered _for a week,_ along with the _declarations of encouragement_ at the end of each reading. I have preferred the King James Version for scripture that I cite here – you should also refer to the version that speaks to you most clearly.

I hope that peace, encouragement and some measure of guidance will be the result of this reading, even as the challenges and triumphs of life press on. Please allow yourself to float into the subject matter and go _"hmmm...food for thought"._

Michael U. Anthony

Read Me First

Proverbs 18:21
Death and life are in the power of the tongue: and they that love it shall eat the fruit thereof.

Take a moment to ponder the immense scope of these words of scripture, the infallible Word of God. Then REMEMBER, "It applies to me! Yes, me! There is so much potential to affect the direction of my life and it's hidden in plain sight in the Word of God. This is a manifestation of His great Love in a way not expressed anywhere else."

Job 22:25-30
[25] *Yea, the Almighty shall be thy defence, and thou shalt have plenty of silver.*
[26] *For then shalt thou have thy delight in the Almighty, and shalt lift up thy face unto God.*
[27] *Thou shalt make thy prayer unto him, and he shall hear thee, and thou shalt pay thy vows.*
[28] *Thou shalt also decree a thing, and it shall be established unto thee: and the light shall shine upon thy ways.*
[29] *When men are cast down, then thou shalt say, There is lifting up; and he shall save the humble person.*
[30] *He shall deliver the island of the innocent: and it is delivered by the pureness of thine hands.*

These verses give us the instructions and results of a life empowered by the Holy Spirit *through* regeneration by Jesus's blood. It brings further clarity to the Truth found in Proverbs 18:21. The choice is ours regarding the direction of our declaration, however as Joshua said, "...but as for me and my house, we will serve the Lord".

At the end of each reading, there is a ***declaration of encouragement***. This should be used daily to build up Hope, Faith and Trust. **Declarations** should be scripture-based and are tailored for the myriad experiences we meet. You are encouraged to write **declarations** that fit your particular situation, and see the Lord work as you put His precepts to work for you.

Do not miss the concept that you can actually speak (***declare***) until things change. Whether it be a sickness, situation, project, hope, dream or any of the myriad ever-changing scenes of life, the power of the spoken word is a treasure available to all.

Christmas, Palm Sunday, Easter

As with every established religion, the Christian faith is very much about its traditions, seasons and holy days, as they unite contemporary Christians the world over.

The Lenten season begins 40 days before Easter Sunday and is a period of introspection, spiritual cleansing and preparation for Easter. Lent is traditionally about giving something up – generally something meaningful to the individual and representative of a sacrifice. This mimics the sacrifice of Jesus Christ for us.

Palm Sunday is one week before Easter and marks Jesus Christ's arrival into Jerusalem. Jesus had been teaching for three years by that time, continuously downplaying his roles of Messiah, Healer and Teacher.

The Thursday before Easter – Maundy Thursday – was the day of the Last Supper of Christ with his disciples. Good Friday was the day of his crucifixion. The third day after that, Easter Sunday, was the day he rose from the dead.

Although for many Christians Christmas seems to be the most popular of holy days, without argument Easter is the most important Holy Day of the Christian faith. The resurrection of Jesus is, indeed, the core event of Christianity. His resurrection really supports his declared authority, his ability to die for the sins of mankind, and speaks volumes to us about eternity and eternal life.

Let Not Your Heart Be Troubled – Christmas

John 14:1

Let not your heart be troubled: ye believe in God, believe also in Me.

Matthew 1:18

Now the birth of Jesus Christ was on this wise: When as his mother Mary was espoused to Joseph, before they came together, she was found with child of the Holy Ghost.

Matthew 2 [Full Chapter]

Now when Jesus was born in Bethlehem of Judaea in the days of Herod the king, behold, there came wise men from the east to Jerusalem, Saying, Where is he that is born King of the Jews? for we have seen his star in the east, and are come to worship him. When Herod the king had heard these things, he was troubled, and all Jerusalem with him. ...

The real power of what Christmas means is not found in the gift giving and merriment, although these are acts of goodwill and are vital and necessary parts of our humanity – and of our celebration of Christmas!

The real power of Christmas is found in what it brought to us in *access* to the Throne of God and the constant *power* released to us through Jesus Christ the Lord.

In our text, Jesus is saying, 'Let not your heart be troubled.' Do you know what a powerful statement that is? This is not simply a friend saying 'don't worry'. This is the Lord Jesus Christ saying not to worry, not to be afraid or fearful, not to get anxious about anything, not to lose hope, not to despair, not to try to accomplish anything according to our human ability – because He is with us. Instead, be calm and peaceful, through faith and belief in God, through Jesus Christ our Lord.

We should instead focus and take full advantage of what the access to and power of the Throne of God brings and gives to us, and when we see this, we will truly 'let not our hearts be troubled'.

I tell you that this nugget of truth is what the real power of Christmas has brought to us. When we grab hold of this, then the goodwill and peace will flow from us and into us. Because we will now have a trouble-free heart to bless and love others. Notice that the problems will still be around, but now handled from the perspective of Faith and the power of access to the Throne of God. That means they will not be the consuming factor that before had our hearts troubled, because as we walk in this faith we know that the problems must be – are – solved.

That is why 'without faith it is impossible to please God'. He knows and understands what he has set up for us – to live stress free with trouble-free hearts. But we run along every day and do just the opposite! We worry, worry, worry, and fret, fret, fret, and use our own tongues to confess negative things in life instead of speaking words of faith.

But all of that does not change the truth of the Word of God. It is always waiting for us to come into line with it. So this Christmas season, begin to line yourself up with the Word of God. Speak a word of faith instead of a word of doom and discouragement. Let faith answer your worries and troubles and allow your heart to be trouble-free. Believe in God as the Lord Jesus Christ encourages us to do – after all, He came to give us this message and so much more.

So as you go along this Christmas season and the things and news of life seems to want to overwhelm you, practice the faith brought to earth by our Lord Jesus Christ. Not that the negative things will not be there, but that you will use what Jesus told us to do to handle them. Let the faith provided by our Lord Jesus Christ be our focus and let not your hearts be troubled. It is at least worth a try, since Jesus came all the way to earth to bring the message.

> *I declare* *that the Peace and Goodwill ushered in on that first Christmas will be my portion on a daily basis. I will make the decision each day to allow the gifts of Peace and Goodwill to overcome all obstacles and discouraging situations, as I reach for Christ's Love by faith through Belief in my heart and Confession in prayer.*

Are We Worthy? – Lent

> **Genesis 32:9-10**
> *⁹ And Jacob said, O God of my father Abraham, and God of my father Isaac, the Lord which saidst unto me, Return unto thy country, and to thy kindred, and I will deal well with thee:*
> *¹⁰ I am not worthy of the least of all the mercies, and of all the truth, which thou hast shewed unto thy servant; for with my staff I passed over this Jordan; and now I am become two bands.*

Lent is when the believer examines his life as a Christian through prayer, penance and repentance of sins, doing good works, atonement, and self-denial. Lent does not have to occur only during our Christian Lenten season. It can be a Christian's response throughout the year. As we contemplate, in our Lenten practices, the sacrifice of God's son Jesus for our redemption, let us look for a moment at our side of the picture.

We are all very familiar with the price that Jesus paid for us to be restored to right relationship with God and not only restored from Adam's fall, but to have that access to restoration without the formalities of animal sacrifice, priests and all the like. Yes, Jesus paid it all – but the question is, *Are we worth it*?

Are we worth the price He paid; do we deserve it? Was it owed to us? Is it something that He had to do?

Sometimes the way we act and behave, you would think that not only our fellowman, but God Himself, had to do whatever it took to save us. If we look at mankind generally, the conclusion must be drawn that the attitude of *He had to do it* is what is driving them.

If this were not the case, why then the putting off of repentance, why then the willful and degrading sinful lifestyles, the child molestations, the blatant adultery, the disobedience to those in authority (home, school, government and especially church) – why is the world saying to God, "You had to do it"? This is very troubling and grievous to the Holy Spirit and to caring and loving Christians.

The Word of God tells us that *our righteousness is as filthy rags in the sight of God.* This alone should make us realize that NO! We are not worth it! NO! We do not deserve it! The Grace, Mercy and Great Love of God is what has kept this sinful generation alive.

The warning is going forth today: Stop living as if you deserve to live; make confession; repent and say like Jacob of old from a truly contrite heart. "*I am not worthy of the least of all the mercies, and of all the truth, which thou hast shewed unto thy servant.*" Make today your Lent of penance and repentance, of atonement.

Until we as individuals come to the place where we get the perspective of how important it is to truly revere the Lord God, we will continue to act out our lives in a manner that says, 'I am worth it, and He had to do it'. This is a seriously mistaken position to have, but I pray today that we will begin to see ourselves as nothing in His sight and His righteousness as all we need.

> *I declare* that from this day forward I will adjust my attitude to a place of humility and obedience to God's Word. I realize that God resists the proud and gives grace to the humble. I also realize that "pride goeth before destruction and a haughty spirit before a fall."

The Irony in Palm Sunday

John 12:12-13

2 On the next day much people that were come to the feast, when they heard that Jesus was coming to Jerusalem,
13 Took branches of palm trees, and went forth to meet him, and cried, Hosanna: Blessed is the King of Israel that cometh in the name of the Lord.

John 18:38-4

38 Pilate saith unto him, What is truth? And when he had said this, he went out again unto the Jews, and saith unto them, I find in him no fault at all.
39 But ye have a custom, that I should release unto you one at the passover: will ye therefore that I release unto you the King of the Jews?
40 Then cried they all again, saying, Not this man, but Barabbas. Now Barabbas was a robber.

John 19:6

When the chief priests therefore and officers saw him, they cried out, saying, Crucify him, crucify him. Pilate saith unto them, Take ye him, and crucify him: for I find no fault in him.

The irony in Palm Sunday is a true replica of the irony in life for those who will live for and tell only the real truth.

Jesus had such a life, for on his triumphal entry into Jerusalem (which we now commemorate as *Palm Sunday*), Jesus was making the final steps towards the completion of his plan to redeem man to God. The same people who were praising him and naming him as 'King of Israel' would be the same people to later say 'Crucify him!' Isn't that ironic? Yet it is so true how in life we can give our very lives in trying to serve, help and deliver people, and then these same people turn on us shortly there-after and say 'away with you' … They crucify you!

In Jesus' case, we find the ironic twist in **John chapter 18:38-40** and **chapter 19:6**. He spent his entire ministry healing, delivering, raising from the dead, forgiving, teaching the truth about holy living, and still, after hav-ing enjoyed the benefits of that ministry for a while, they cried, 'Crucify him!'

You see the reason is that although the truth that is being told is for their salvation, people often 'shoot the messenger' of the real truth – preferring a safer, watered down, compromising version of what it really takes to meet a Holy God. So we will find that when told that adultery, divorce, remarriage (for just any reason) is wrong … that all dishonesty, lying, deception, jealousy, hatred, greed, envy and especially unforgive-ness is wrong … you will be sentenced to crucifixion, although you are trying to save their lives.

Isn't it healthy to come face to face with the reality of life? To face the fact that life is full of ironies at all levels? The truth is that the irony of Palm Sunday points to the irony of life in general. But this same Jesus will not deal with you in an ironic or hypocritical way! If you come to Jesus, He will not betray you, He will be with you to the end.

> *I declare* that I will begin to face life from the perspective of reality. Knowing that my thoughts become my choices, my choices become my actions, my actions become my habits and my habits determine my successes or failures in life.

> *I further declare* that I will speak positive, uplifting and realistic words into my life, for death and life truly are in the power of the tongue.

He is Risen – Easter

Luke 24:1-8

[1] Now upon the first day of the week, very early in the morning, they came unto the sepulchre, bringing the spices which they had prepared, and certain others with them.
[2] And they found the stone rolled away from the sepulchre.
[3] And they entered in, and found not the body of the Lord Jesus.
[4] And it came to pass, as they were much perplexed thereabout, behold, two men stood by them in shining garments:
[5] And as they were afraid, and bowed down their faces to the earth, they said unto them, Why seek ye the living among the dead?
[6] He is not here, but is risen: remember how he spake unto you when he was yet in Galilee,
[7] Saying, The Son of man must be delivered into the hands of sinful men, and be crucified, and the third day rise again.
[8] And they remembered his words

The proof of the real God is in the resurrection. He is alive! Hallelujah!

He said that He would do it and He did. All other Gods and religions are put to shame and silence because they cannot go where Jesus went and come back again. He went through death and hell, and came back victoriously with the keys of death and hell. None other can make that claim. As a matter of fact, none other can claim that when called they answer. Remember Elijah on Mount Carmel facing the 400 prophets of Baal? Remember which God answered by fire? Our Lord and God answered and has always answered, and will always continue to answer. Whether it be by fire, healing, deliverance … or simply achieving the impossible, He will answer.

He has given us the power of access to the Throne of God. We now come boldly, pray directly, and get our answers individually. No longer are we handing our chances over to the hand of a Priest or a ritual; we have access because He is risen. Hallelujah!

He is risen as He said He would, but the question is, "Is He risen in your heart?"

> *I **declare** that the crucifixion and resurrection were real and provided access to the Throne of Grace for me!*

> *I **confess** the Lord Jesus and I believe in my heart that God raised Jesus from the dead, and **I declare** my need of salvation in Jesus' name.*

> *I **further declare** that I will continue to pray until His Spirit witnesses with my spirit that I am saved.*

New Year, New Starts, First Things First and Renewal

A personal, spiritual awakening is available to each one of us. As we look back over historical time, often a feeling that we are in a deep hole and cannot dig ourselves out precedes this awakening – which I could also call a renewal of our spirit in Christ.

Sometimes it will come when we realize that we are not alone in praying for a certain type of outcome, and that there is a spiritual community right here for us in this secular world. And then again, sometimes an individual's awakening and renewal comes in answer to the persistent and heart-wrenching question, "Is this all there is for me in this life?"

Welcome any type of renewal, awakening and return to Jesus the Christ that is presented to you!

New Year

Ecclesiastes 3:1-9

[1] *To every thing there is a season, and a time to every purpose under the heaven:*

[2] *A time to be born, and a time to die; a time to plant, and a time to pluck up that which is planted;*

[3] *A time to kill, and a time to heal; a time to break down, and a time to build up;*

[4] *A time to weep, and a time to laugh; a time to mourn, and a time to dance;*

[5] *A time to cast away stones, and a time to gather stones together; a time to embrace, and a time to refrain from embracing;*

[6] *A time to get, and a time to lose; a time to keep, and a time to cast away;*

[7] *A time to rend, and a time to sew; a time to keep silence, and a time to speak;*

[8] *A time to love, and a time to hate; a time of war, and a time of peace.*

[9] *What profit hath he that worketh in that wherein he laboureth?*

As we enter into any New Year, this is the time we most often take a moment – or perhaps longer than a moment – to reflect on the failures and successes of the past year or years, and to plan or make resolutions for the New Year.

This is because the New Year offers us a point in time to take a breather and start anew. Now, if we really consider it, this is nothing more than just another day we have been allowed to live. But the calendar which separates the days has marked this out as our New Year's Day, and so we live by that distinction and make decisions surrounding this particular day that will impact the rest of the year.

I want more to talk to you this morning than to preach, and as we look at our scripture text in **Ecclesiastes 3:1-9**, we find that our best approach to life is one of being realistic in nature. We must be realistic in the truth that as much as we plan, life will bring about a surprising number of unexpected factors and events. Things that we do not have in our plans.

Most people make plans for only the good and positive things in life and so when a negative happens we are taken as if by surprise. We act as if this should never have happened and we blame God. But the Word of God tells us clearly that both good and bad have their perfect time and season. Thus, the prudent person will plan for the eventuality of both.

Let's get serious: How many of you plan, or put aside finances specifically for accidents, sickness, and death? I believe not many do. We'd rather concentrate on parties, celebrations and other niceties, but the reality is we need to come face to face with all the areas of life. We need to plan and live with the expectation of both good and bad coming along at sometime or the other. When something negative does happen it will not take us under, because we had our own contingency plan.

If we read the scripture in **Ecclesiastes 3:1-9** carefully, that is what it is telling us: expect both the good and the bad and be prepared to face both. For as long as you are alive, both will come along sooner or later. It was Job who said, "Shall we expect good only at the hand of the Lord and not evil?" My encouragement to you is to live a life of realistic expectations this year and not a life of fanciful, unreal imaginations.

Remember that with the Lord Jesus Christ you can face all the realities of life. Whether they be good or bad, put your trust in Him. Job kept his trust in the Lord and made it through the good and bad, and so can you.

Happy and Realistic New Year!

> *I declare that all of my disappointments will become divine appointments!*

> *I declare that I will be the head and not the tail, above and not beneath, a victor and not a victim.*

> *I declare that I am blessed in my going out and coming in, my uprising and my down-sitting, I'm blessed in the city and blessed in the field!*

Speak the Word

Proverbs 18:21
21 Death and life are in the power of the tongue: and they that love it shall eat the fruit thereof.

Romans 10:10
10 For with the heart man believeth unto righteousness; and with the mouth confession is made unto salvation.

Matthew 12:36-37
36 But I say unto you, That every idle word that men shall speak, they shall give account thereof in the day of judgment.
37 For by thy words thou shalt be justified, and by thy words thou shalt be condemned.

The power of the spoken word has been under-appreciated, under-valued, misused in too many circumstances, and unused when it would have been appropriate.

The spoken word has started wars. Healed broken relationships. Given relief to those under oppression. Created vows that are binding in marriage.

The spoken word hurts, helps, heals, gives hope, joy, peace, sadness and so much more. The spoken word is our primary means of communication. In fact, without the spoken word, I could not reach you in this particular medium (radio, in this original talk) today.

Our theme song for this broadcast says, 'We need a word from you, if we don't hear from you what shall we do?' Of course, this is the particular request made of the Lord, but we hunger and thirst for the spoken word. In fact, the spoken word is so powerful that the Bible places it in the correct context in **Proverbs 18:21** *"Death and life are in the power of the tongue."*

I submit to you that not only physical life and death, but spiritual life and death, are in the power of the tongue, the life and death of your friendships and relationships, marriages, associations, businesses and all other matters are in the power of the tongue. The Word of God is pointing out to us that with our voice, we build up walls and break down walls. These walls are emotional, spiritual and psychological structures placed there by the words that come from our tongue – walls of unforgiveness, walls of hatred, walls of envy, walls of jealousy, walls of bitterness and walls of misunderstanding and all that ever springs from such things.

With our tongue, we destroy potential in our young people, hinder progress of others, and often times kill many dreams of our future potential leaders, simply because we do not realize the power of the spoken word, especially when used in the wrong context, and when intending to hurt and demoralize others.

But, thank God we can, with the same tongue, correct the hurts and the wrongs, with the same tongue we can bring healing to the wounds, with the same tongue we can explain the misunderstandings, with the same tongue we can break down all of the walls. There is so much potential in what the Lord has provided for us, all we have to do is to make use of it ... with the correct words on our tongue, with the right voice.

The power of the spoken word is so great that the Bible instructs us in **Romans 10:10** *"For with the heart man believeth unto righteousness; and with the mouth confession is made unto salvation."* Do you see that, even the miracle of salvation is hinged upon the confession of the word?

Let me tell you, the spoken word is powerful! We need to appreciate the great importance of it in our lives and relationships. Let us begin to practice from today. As we put God first and keep him there, as we develop our desire for God, we will confess that desire. We will confess keeping God first. We will confess positive things. We will speak blessings and not curses, praise and not criticism. We will come the realization that our words are the instruments of death and life!

It is a great responsibility that the Lord has placed upon us to be good stewards of the words we speak. Remember we must give an account for every idle word spoken. Let's begin afresh and commit to using the word for life, joy, love – and not for death, misery or criticism. Read **Matthew 12:36-37** once again.

> *I declare* to commence speaking words of life, healing, forgiveness, deliverance and positive direction.

> *I declare* that I will cast down imaginations and every high thing that exalts itself against the knowledge of God, and bring every thought captive to the obedience of Christ.

Renew

Romans 12:1-2

[1] *I beseech you therefore, brethren, by the mercies of God, that ye present your bodies a living sacrifice, holy, acceptable unto God, which is your reasonable service.*
[2] *And be not conformed to this world: but be ye transformed by the renewing of your mind, that ye may prove what is that good, and acceptable, and perfect, will of God.*

Genesis 6:6

And it repented the Lord that he had made man on the earth, and it grieved him at his heart.

Romans 12:20-21

[20] *Therefore if thine enemy hunger, feed him; if he thirst, give him drink: for in so doing thou shalt heap coals of fire on his head.*
[21] *Be not overcome of evil, but overcome evil with good.*

The struggle to do right is constantly going on within us. That is an accurate description of the human race coming from the Maker. The truth of the matter is, although we will not admit it, we all have some unholy thoughts and make our share of unfortunate decisions, and denying this does not change the fact of the truth of it.

Now, we have been down this road before, but it bears repeating. The human is a combination of many things, but the one thing that is needed to bring all other things into correct order is a stable mind. More valuable than just a stable mind is a **renewed mind**, there is only one way for renewal of the mind, and that is through the blood of the Lord Jesus Christ.

You see, a stable mind allows you to make good moral decisions, but a renewed mind in addition to that, allows you to come to Christ-like decisions that often times do not line up with the accepted morally correct, although it is 'Godly' correct.

For example, today the accepted morality of the world says that it is okay to "do unto the enemy as he has done unto you". But the renewed mind in Christ says, "I will prove the greater love of God" and do as **Romans 12:20-21** says. I will overcome evil with good, react to hatred with love.

> *I declare* *that I will use my God-given ability to be creative and not destructive, forgiving and not bitter, overcoming evil by demonstrating good.*

> *I declare* *that my example will be pleasing to God and beneficial to my fellowman.*

Waiting

Isaiah 40:31

[31] *But they that wait upon the* Lord *shall renew their strength; they shall mount up with wings as eagles; they shall run, and not be weary; and they shall walk, and not faint.*

Waiting is not simply sitting down! It is a waiting with a joyful expectation, a calm assurance that the result will be joy and peace. Waiting is often a test of our faith!

It is like when you are at the airport waiting for the arrival of someone. Although the flight might be delayed, you know that the end result will be that the plane will arrive and that you will have a joyful meeting with that person.

So it is when we wait upon the Lord – except the test comes when we doubt His 'plane' will actually arrive, so to speak. We wait, at best, with a joyful expectation, fully confident and knowing that the Lord will come through for us. We wait and keep on praying. Though it may sometimes seem like He tarries, He will come through on time – and above and beyond our expectations.

The waiting of the world is full of worry, doubt and fear, and is a dreadful thing. But the Lord our God will answer and He will answer speedily for those who wait in faith on Him. Whatever the decision that you are contemplating, wait quietly for the answer from the Lord. It is a good way to strengthen and renew your faith.

I declare that I will develop an attitude of waiting with a joyful expectation. I will not become anxious for anything; rather, **I will prayerfully make** my requests known unto God with thanksgiving.

I know that patience will make me perfect and entire and **I decide** to mature in this manner!

Attitudes, Assumptions and Feelings

Meditating with Christ, reading your Bible and praying are three ways that any one of us is able to correct wrong attitudes, mistaken assumptions and negative feelings that may at any time overwhelm us.

Feeling sorry for ourselves or wringing our hands with anxiety and worry are two examples of negative feelings that we can surrender to Christ. The mistaken assumption that we are all alone in the world, purposeless and abandoned by all is incorrect, simply because Christ is always with us.

We do, however, need to turn to Christ in our meditations and prayers. We can correct our mistaken assumptions by finding the truth held in the Bible. We can assume an attitude that, "All problems are resolved through Christ and all is possible through Him."

Assumption

1 Corinthians 10:12

12 Wherefore let him that thinketh he standeth take heed, lest he fall.

Assumptions are a good thing in doing research and scientific experiments, for scientists need to start somewhere – so they make assumptions to test certain theories that have not already been proven. Now, that is good for that area of life, but when it comes to the realities of everyday life and the hope of heaven, assumptions are just not the way to proceed! We have to go with the proven way, and Jesus said that it is this, *"I am the way, the truth and the life; no man cometh unto the Father but by me."*

You see if a scientist makes an incorrect assumption (and they often do), the solution is to simply re-run the test or conduct the experiment again until the expected or desired results are obtained. But in life we have a one-shot deal, no second chances. The scientists can try and try again just as students trying to pass a test can try again, but once we die, that's it. We have no second chance, we must make sure that we die in the correct posture with Jesus Christ our Lord. If we miss heaven once we have missed it all forever, that is why assumptions in life and especially about eternal life are so critically dangerous, that is why we MUST, I say MUST make our wrongs right and our crooked paths straight NOW!

We cannot afford to spoil our one-shot deal with the assumption that we will be accepted by the Lord without doing what He has required as necessary.

Our scripture verse is a warning against assumptions. Read it again. You may think or imagine that you're standing upright – but Corinthians says that maybe you are not! Don't assume. Check it the reality of your circumstances. If you don't, you might risk a fall.

You see the dangerous thing about assumptions is that you can become comfortable in the wrong position. Now that is making a bad story worse, because you are wrong in the first place and then assume that it will be okay if you just ignore it and carry on. This leads to complacency and soon it feels comfortable to leave it as it is, unresolved.

I am here to tell you that the only way to fix our problems is to face them, and by that I mean facing the reality of it. Assuming that they will just go away is to fulfill our scripture verse and risk that fall. And worse yet – to take the unnecessary chance on a one-shot life.

My dear readers, life is too short and eternity is too long to face, based on an assumption. Let me encourage you today, not tomorrow but today, to face your challenges and problems very carefully, honestly and very prayerfully, but face them you must! They will not go away with an assumption and when you think that you are standing on good ground, you might just end up falling. This can be avoided by taking concrete steps on the proven ground found in the teaching of the Bible and in relationship with the Lord Jesus Christ. Let the Lord have his way with you today for eternal assurance and also face your life situations today so that you may stand and not fall.

> *I declare* that I will take a somber moment to carefully consider my eternal destiny.

> *I declare* that neither friends, family, foes, fame, fortune, circumstances or position is worth missing my eternal destiny promised in Christ Jesus.

Does God Hate Me?

Ephesians 2:1-5

[1] And you hath he quickened, who were dead in trespasses and sins;

[2] Wherein in time past ye walked according to the course of this world, according to the prince of the power of the air, the spirit that now worketh in the children of disobedience:

[3] Among whom also we all had our conversation in times past in the lusts of our flesh, fulfilling the desires of the flesh and of the mind; and were by nature the children of wrath, even as others.

[4] But God, who is rich in mercy, for his great love wherewith he loved us,

[5] Even when we were dead in sins, hath quickened us together with Christ, (by grace ye are saved;)

1 Corinthians 2:5-14

[5] That your faith should not stand in the wisdom of men, but in the power of God.

[6] Howbeit we speak wisdom among them that are perfect: yet not the wisdom of this world, nor of the princes of this world, that come to nought:

[7] But we speak the wisdom of God in a mystery, even the hidden wisdom, which God ordained before the world unto our glory:

[8] Which none of the princes of this world knew: for had they known it, they would not have crucified the Lord of glory.

[9] But as it is written, eye hath not seen, nor ear heard, neither have entered into the heart of man, the things which God hath prepared for them that love him.

[10] But God hath revealed them unto us by his Spirit: for the Spirit searcheth all things, yea, the deep things of God.

[11] For what man knoweth the things of a man, save the spirit of man which is in him? even so the things of God knoweth no man, but the Spirit of God.

[12] Now we have received, not the spirit of the world, but the spirit which is of God; that we might know the things that are freely given to us of God.

[13] Which things also we speak, not in the words which man's wisdom teacheth, but which the Holy Ghost teacheth; comparing spiritual things with spiritual.

[14] But the natural man receiveth not the things of the Spirit of God: for they are foolishness unto him: neither can he know them, because they are spiritually discerned.

Job 23:8-10

[8] Behold, I go forward, but he is not there; and backward, but I cannot perceive him:

[9] On the left hand, where he doth work, but I cannot behold him: he hideth himself on the right hand, that I cannot see him:

[10] But he knoweth the way that I take: when he hath tried me, I shall come forth as gold.

Jeremiah 29:11

[11] For I know the thoughts that I think toward you, saith the LORD, thoughts of peace, and not of evil, to give you an expected end.

Did He change? Why do I have so many issues in my life? What about His promises?

Is it because God hates me?

In our life, there are many perplexing circumstances which often leave a "Godless" feeling. That empty, hopeless, vacuum of non-connection is a dreaded situation for any human. A sense of loss in relation to God. A sense of separation. Job had this experience of missing God.

The overwhelming circumstances of this life can bring even the best of us to the point of asking the unthinkable. Humans turn to their emotions and ask, "Does God hate me?" or "Is He gone?" Our bleak feelings block out the "God loves us" words of this scripture!

A natural reaction when seeking an explanation about the ways of the Infinite Lord is to attempt to formulate something that is satisfying (or even understandable) to our *finite* minds. And we are stuck again.

Let us think about this for a moment. If God hated us, what's to stop Him from immediately destroying us? Who can withstand God? Why would He allow us to live if He hated us? Does He find pleasure in our suffering? Our human nature finds it hard to reconcile with God's love.

The Lord knows us more intimately than we could ever know ourselves. The key to learning the lessons of maturity in our walk with the Lord is to allow our Faith to stand in His power, being assured that He does not hate us, but lovingly guides us through the difficulties as we exercise faith and gain the victory through Him.

> *I declare that instead of finding excuses to justify God's seeming hatred, I will find hope and faith in the expressions of Love, Joy, Hope and Peace found in His promises in the Bible. I decide to accept His Love above my feelings of rejection!*

Regrets

Genesis 6:5-6
[5] *And God saw that the wickedness of man was great in the earth, and that every imagination of the thoughts of his heart was only evil continually.*
[6] *And it repented the Lord that he had made man on the earth, and it grieved him at his heart.*

We all have any number of things that we would rather change in life. They are called regrets, and grief accompanies regrets.

The truth about life is that you can never go back to change what happened. We only go forward or remain stagnant. So, as we look at the best option for possible change available to us, we realize that to remain stagnant is to give up and die, so we *must* move forward. In our moving forward, while we cannot go back and change the things of the past, we can move forward in a manner that lessens their effects upon us. We can _try_ to avoid the same or similar regretful actions or situations in our today.

The only tool we have to let us deal with change is the present moment and our actions now. So what we have, as we deal with our regrets, is the future built by us in each present moment. To put it simply, we only have today and that is true every day. We cannot wait for some utopian day to come; we must act in each day we live because this day in which we live is really our future. Therefore, the argument of putting off and procrastinating is put to death! We must make the change today. The excuse of tomorrow does not work. Change today!

The saddest thing about regrets is the failure to learn from them and to choose something different from now on.

Those who fail to learn from and change their today as a result of regrets are doomed in a very real way to remain stagnant. The saddest thing about being stagnant is to not realize that you are in a state of real regression, and this failure is best described as denial.

So it is with our spiritual life: quite often people know that they need to change but they always say "tomorrow". They realize that action only takes place in our today. These people end up in a state of regression and constant denial, and come to the end of their today (which is their life) and never change.

After God's regret of making man, He put an avenue of change into place through Jesus Christ our Lord. For through the power of Jesus Christ, man can overcome the evil thoughts that made God regret making him. We ought to follow God's example and put our strategies for change into place. We need to begin with placing Jesus Christ as the LORD of our life, not in pretense, but in fact.

My encouragement to you is to make the most of your today, beginning with each morning, and moment by moment resolve to make a change.

If you have been guilty of mismanagement of your parental responsibilities, change. If you have been neglectful of meaningful relationships on any level, change. If you have been taking things for granted and regretted when they ended up negative, change. If you have been assuming the Lord Jesus Christ is just for tomorrow, change – by calling Him in right now. If you have been a liar, thief, cheat, deceiver – change!

In short, be realistic, shake off the dust of regret, open your eyes to present day truth and make the necessary changes today. For there is only hope in tomorrow; action can only take place in our today. The only time to correct regrets is today. If we come to the end and still have unresolved regrets, it will mean that we failed to take hold of today. It will mean that we bet too heavily on the elusive tomorrow! *That* will be the ultimate regret – that we lost that bet.

We all know that the ultimate regret is to die without making the change into Christ Jesus as personal Lord and Savior.

> *I declare* that all of my regrets will become stepping stones to victories.

> *I declare* that I will use my freedom to choose and make choices which turn my sorrows in joy. I will turn my failures into new opportunities. I will change my pathway away from destruction and into salvation.

The Valley of the Shadow

Psalm 23:4

Yea, though I walk through the valley of the shadow of death, I will fear no evil: for thou art with me; thy rod and thy staff they comfort me.

The thing that grabs us most about this verse of scripture is the reality of the words. The Psalmist David does not try to live in a fantasy world. He acknowledges right away that YES, I walk through the valley of the shadow of death. Now this gives us the picture of dark and gloomy times and harsh seasons. A season in life in which the atmosphere around you is overshadowed by the despair and darkness cast by death which seems to be looming over everything. It gives the sense of foreboding evil taking over, but through it we must go. To get to where we need to be, to get to the place that the Lord has called us to be, to fulfill our purpose in life, we must pass through this valley.

Let us take special note that the valley or season in life is not death itself, but merely has the pall of death or the effects of death hanging over it. This should tell us that this is not a place in which we will die, but rather a place of testing our resolve to press through what seems to be the darkest of times, seasons, and places. This is the place where we join with David and say, *I will fear no evil, for thou are with me*. This is the place of confidence building, faith building, character building, a place where only the Lord can bring you out, only the Lord can deliver, only the Lord can answer. This is not the place where you give up and die, although the enemy represented by the words fear and evil would want it to be so. This is the place where you say because I know that the Lord is with me, I am fully persuaded that I will get through this, I shall live and not die and proclaim the goodness of the Lord.

To know that Lord is with me is the key to success in this situation. To know is far different from believing. You can believe something but not have the proof or experience that it is actually so. For example, I can believe that the fire is hot and will burn me, but when I actually touch fire and it burns me, I will have a different perspective and my confession and actions will be based upon experience and hard knowledge rather than on the speculation of simply believing that it is so. That is how it is with knowing that the Lord is with you. Do you know what it is to have confidence? Well, there is no better or greater confidence than the confidence of knowing that the Lord is with you. That confidence is what took David through the valley and it is what will take you through. Remember the valley is the place of confidence building, not a place of death. Challenge, yes – but Man has always survived challenges. And come through the stronger for it.

Today I want us all to sit a while, lie down a while, wait a while and really consider the message here today, that *I know the Lord is with me*. Just reflect on all of what that means to each of us individually. There are a lot of things that we know, but do we really realize what it means to Know the Lord is with me?

> ***I declare*** *that I will no longer operate from a place of simply belief; rather I will acquire the confidence gained from the knowledge that experience brings and operate in that confidence.*

> ***I also declare*** *I know that the Lord is with me and therefore I fear no appearance of evil.*

The Truth about the Spirit of Fear

2 Timothy 1:7
For God hath not given us the spirit of fear; but of power, and of love, and of a sound mind.

1 John 4:18
There is no fear in love; but perfect love casteth out fear: because fear hath torment. He that feareth is not made perfect in love.

Fear is not from God. We could say that fear is a spirit and not really an emotion that is real. As the children say, FEAR = False Evidence Appearing Real. Yet the Lord understands how strong a hold fear has over His children, because there are 110 places in the Bible where we are exhorted to "fear not" or "be not afraid."

Our ordinary minds – our fearful humanness – uses fear to cripple and bind us, to hinder us in our endeavors, and to keep us from our potential in Christ. In short, fear – from the extreme panic attack to the mildest nervousness – torments us!

Cave into fear, and you become its slave. At its deepest source, all fear is based on the fear of death and dying. We look at our mortality rather than at our eternity when we are caving in to fear. We look away from the Lord and the devil likes it like that! Fear is a tool, a weapon in the devil's very war against the fulfillment of the Lord's promises to you for your life.

And here, dear reader, is your power! You are the *master* over this spirit of fear. Ah, yes! It may have a spiritual stranglehold on your life, but you can decide to pull it down – decide, with a prayer that the Lord lends assistance to you to be done with fear!

To pull down and bind your fear, or to cast it out from your experience forever, call on the love of God with great commitment and determination! God provides perfected love and His love acts on fear just as light acts on darkness. Just as a tiny little flame of a single candle erases the darkness, so does the quietest expression of love eradicate your fear.

To keep fear away, confess and believe the word of God in a daily application to your life – and do so with total faith and confidence. You are redeemed and have the right in Christ to live free of the curse of fear. Sing thus and praise the Lord, thanking him for his blessings in your daily life.

> Rather than fear, **I declare**, "Bless the Lord O my soul, Bless his Holy Name, I receive all of His benefits and I forget them not, I am redeemed from the curse of fear, I am redeemed from anything or anyone who tries in any way to hurt or harm me. I am redeemed, let the redeemed of the Lord say so!"

Youth, Old-Age and Eternal Life

Youth can be lived with a fearless brazenness, just as it might be lived in purposeless despair.

As we come into adult age, we tend to focus on things of the world – a job or career, building wealth or accumulating possessions, starting a family – rather than on things of the heart, spirit and Christ.

And then, as our hair turns gray and we notice that our body does not have its youthful strength anymore, we may tremble with fear about what old age has in store for us. We may worry about who will care for us or how it will be paid for.

From youngest youth to oldest age, guidance and confidence resides in Christ Jesus, in communion with Him and those around you who trust in Him.

Your Attitude is What Counts

Matthew 19:20-26

[20] *The young man saith unto him, All these things have I kept from my youth up: what lack I yet?*

[21] *Jesus said unto him, If thou wilt be perfect, go and sell that thou hast, and give to the poor, and thou shalt have treasure in heaven: and come and follow me.*

[22] *But when the young man heard that saying, he went away sorrowful: for he had great possessions.*

[23] *Then said Jesus unto his disciples, Verily I say unto you, That a rich man shall hardly enter into the kingdom of heaven.*

[24] *And again I say unto you, It is easier for a camel to go through the eye of a needle, than for a rich man to enter into the kingdom of God.*

[25] *When his disciples heard it, they were exceedingly amazed, saying, Who then can be saved?*

[26] *But Jesus beheld them, and said unto them, With men this is impossible; but with God all things are possible.*

Our attitude is not just a reaction but indeed it is our outlook or perspective concerning the various issues of life. It can also be described as the position we take and the behaviors we express in face of the issues and challenges that life brings.

In our text today, the young man (commonly referred to as the *Rich Young Ruler*) started his discourse with Jesus with the correct intention, which was to find the way to eternal life with God. For we all know that we must spend eternity somewhere, either with God in Christ Jesus or in Hell, there are simply no other options. So, he had the right intention of trying to find the right way to be with God.

After listening, Jesus gave him two levels of instruction. First was how to live on earth in a manner pleasing to God and his fellowman. After the young man affirmed that he had fulfilled those requirements, Jesus then answered his deeper concern of what was lacking.

The young man knew that something was lacking in his life and seeking Jesus for the answer was again the right thing to do. However, his *attitude* upon hearing the answer that Jesus gave was what made the difference – it became the turning point.

You see my dear readers, our attitude towards the truth of the Word of God is what causes us to accept or reject it. Please notice that our attitude does change the truth from being what is it (simply the Truth), but our attitude surely does count when it comes to accepting and applying the truth. For we can accept something as truth but fail to apply it to our lives, thereby rendering that truth ineffective in operation in our life. This sadly was the failed position taken by the Rich Young Ruler, for he failed to apply revealed truth to his life. He walked away when he was told to give up all he possessed. His attitude was that it was simply too much to give up, even in exchange for eternal life with God! Now, if we can see how deceived he was – for the things of the earth are but for a moment and all is the Lord's, so when we give it up for Him there is simply much more abundance that He will provide here and now and in eternity everlasting life with Him.

This is an important concept, too often missed by people who manage to somehow get a few nice possessions on earth and think that they have it all or have arrived. It is this false sense of "security in possessions" that Jesus was alluding to when He said it will be easier for a camel to pass through the eye of a needle than for a rich man to enter the kingdom of God. Jesus does not mean that rich folks cannot receive salvation. Anyone who humbles himself, confesses and repents can receive salvation. But the thing is people who are blinded by their possessions often times share the attitude of this Rich Young Ruler. It is too much to give up for the Lord, and this is so rigidly ingrained that it is likened to a camel trying to pass through the eye of a needle.

My dear reader, today do not let this Rich Young Ruler Attitude be yours! Whatever is necessary to let go of for eternal life with God, please let go of it. It may be even just your bad attitude, anger, unforgiveness, hatred, envy, jealousy, or, yes, even your love of and actual possessions. Because in so doing you are showing the Lord that you prefer Him above all else and that is all He wanted from the young man – proof that he pre-ferred Him above all else.

> *I declare* that I will not allow the affections for the tempo-rary things of life or life's debilitating emotional upheavals, to stifle, replace or hinder my love for Christ and the prom-ise of eternal life found in Him.

> *I acknowledge* that with God all things are possible.

Remember Now...

Ecclesiastes 12:1
Remember now thy Creator in the days of thy youth, while the evil days come not, nor the years draw nigh, when thou shalt say, I have no pleasure in them

Psalm 71:5
For thou art my hope, O Lord God: thou art my trust from my youth.

1 Timothy 4:12
Let no man despise thy youth; but be thou an example of the believers, in word, in conversation, in charity, in spirit, in faith, in purity.

We read these words of instruction, and sometimes we may take the message to mean only have a thought about the Lord who created us all and leave it there. (And by the way, go ahead and read the entire chapter 4 of 1st Timothy).

But the message is not one of thought only, but indeed it is one of a *lifestyle*. This means that we must not only think about the Lord Jesus Christ, but we must also put into practice the principles that He taught and lived by as an example for us.

The reason that this is important to do from the days of our youth is that we are building in life a character, a reputation, a methodology, habits, and a way of thinking. We will use this foundation for the rest of our life to make decisions which lead into our place of success or failure.

So it is critical at the foundational stages of life (youth) that our Creator be a major part of the process which will carry us through life. This is not to be ignored or taken lightly, for in the hard reality of life, some things come along in which only a relationship with the Lord Jesus Christ is able to sustain someone and bring some peace and relief. The lack of such a relationship from a young age is the reason so many of the useless alternatives such as drugs, alcohol, illicit relationships and activities are used as an outlet, when the person is really, at their core, looking for peace and relief.

Sadly, too many people find it easier to take the useless alternatives instead of the only sure way which is found in our Creator. But there is still the opportunity of today. There are still the avenues of forgiveness and communication with parents and caring adults who, along with a willing desire by a young person, can help to lead and guide in the right path.

Young people are encouraged to take a few moments to reflect on the positive efforts being made just for their good development, and to begin to appreciate the time and effort being made by caring adults. Let the reward be one of success and purpose for each person. Each of us can be successful very early in life if we have a mind to do so. Remember now ... In the Lord, all things are possible.

> *I declare* *that I will live a life of success based on the truth that my Creator has good thoughts towards me and will give me an expected good end.*

> *I will remember* *my Creator and help someone along the way by revealing these truths to him, and so fulfill the law of Christ.*

Real Rejoicing

Luke 10:19-20

[19] Behold, I give unto you power to tread on serpents and scorpions, and over all the power of the enemy: and nothing shall by any means hurt you.

[20] Notwithstanding in this rejoice not, that the spirits are subject unto you; but rather rejoice, because your names are written in heaven.

So often in life, we focus on the immediate accomplishments and miss the bigger and everlasting eternal focus. In this discourse, the disciples had just experienced the power of invoking the name of Jesus. Their subsequent joy was overwhelming and had the danger of making them lose focus on the eternal importance of their life with Jesus.

So the Master made a statement that brought them back into this focus. Now, we in this day and age make great accomplishments in the name of Jesus, and the message is still the same. Do not lose focus on the things of eternal value as you experience things of temporary value here on earth. For the all things done in the name of Jesus were still at their best *temporary* in the light of eternity. For we need to be reminded of this: that in eternity, rejoicing will come when our name is in the Book of Life in heaven; that rejoicing will last forever, but our present victories will pass away, just as heaven and earth will pass away.

The danger of the wrong focus is to think that we have 'arrived' and have no further need to press forward. A few victories and we lay down the armor, and say, "I've made it to the big leagues; I have achieved it all." The enemy of our souls would like us to think and behave that way, but Jesus who was manifested to destroy the works of the enemy is saying, do not lose focus on the ultimate victory, the ultimate cause for rejoicing. For if we make all the victories and accomplishments in this world, but our names are not written in Heaven, we will learn too late that these accomplishments are temporary and of no value in the eternity that the Lord has promised.

So as we accomplish, and as we achieve, as we do what we have to do in the name of Jesus, remember if our name is not written down in the Book of Life we will have not really accomplished anything at all!

> *I confess* that real rejoicing is that which is described by the Lord Jesus Christ!

> *I declare* that I will do all within my power to ensure that I and others are candidates for real rejoicing by having our names written in heaven where we will rejoice eternally.

Old Age

Psalm 37:23-25

*²³ The steps of a good man are ordered by the L*ORD*: and he delighteth in his way.*
²⁴ Though he fall, he shall not be utterly cast down: for the L*ORD upholdeth him with his hand.*
²⁵ I have been young, and now am old; yet have I not seen the righteous forsaken, nor his seed begging bread.

1 Chronicles 23:1

Now when David reached old age, he made his son Solomon king over Israel.

First of all, old age is not a blessing that many people get to enjoy. Some people die while in their youth, and some of those that live to what we call old age, do so often times in a state that is not healthy, comfortable or enjoyable. Old age is an honor and a blessing that God has poured out on those who are fortunate enough to receive it. Old age is a blessing not only to the long-lived, but to those who interact with persons of old age.

Have you ever had a friendship with a Godly old person? That friendship will bring you much joy, peace, comfort and sound instruction and advice. This is the kind of blessing that God in his sovereignty designed for old age. It comes from a foundation and life based upon a real and meaningful relationship with the Lord Jesus Christ. It is only by investing in their relationship with the Lord that elders can now pour out blessings on those of us who they come into contact with. Being a blessing is not an overnight thing, but it is an outflow of a life of prayer, righteous living and a heart desire to be the best that you can be in whatever area of life you operate.

Sadly, people today do not have very many of these values. Prayer and patience have been replaced by the dollar and technology, and the ultimate sufferer in all this is the soul. You see, so many people have the dollar and have the technology at their fingertips, but if you check a little deeper you will find (and if they are honest enough to admit it) that they are really miserable. They are dissatisfied, unhealthy, untrusting of their partners, fearful, insecure and generally seeking to settle their differences in the courts of law, through counseling or some other social approach that is truly ineffective in giving the soul what it really needs. In short? They are not HAPPY in the Lord.

The soul of man needs peace, a peace that passes all understanding and that peace can only be found in Jesus Christ. It cannot be found in socially acceptable religious affiliations that say to everyone "I go to church every Sunday so that I am judged as godly by my fellowman." You fool no one but yourself! The peace that the soul needs has one source and that is in confession and the resulting continuous relationship with Jesus Christ.

The blessing of an enjoyable old age is set in the foundation of living in Jesus Christ and that foundation needs to start right now.

> *I declare that my trust is in the Lord who has been my stronghold. He will continue to deliver me from troubles and not cast me off in my old age. He will preserve me and I will continue to praise Him as the source of my strength.*

Eternal Life

Matthew 19:16-21

[16] And, behold, one came and said unto him, Good Master, what good thing shall I do, that I may have eternal life?

[17] And he said unto him, Why callest thou me good? There is none good but one, that is, God: but if thou wilt enter into life, keep the commandments.

[18] He saith unto him, Which? Jesus said, Thou shalt do no murder, Thou shalt not commit adultery, Thou shalt not steal, Thou shalt not bear false witness,

[19] Honour thy father and thy mother: and, Thou shalt love thy neighbour as thyself.

[20] The young man saith unto him, All these things have I kept from my youth up: what lack I yet?

[21] Jesus said unto him, If thou wilt be perfect, go and sell that thou hast, and give to the poor, and thou shalt have treasure in heaven: and come and follow me.

John 3:15-16

[15] That whosoever believeth in him should not perish, but have eternal life.

[16] For God so loved the world, that he gave his only begotten Son, that whosoever believeth in him should not perish, but have everlasting life.

John 5:39

[39] Search the scriptures; for in them ye think ye have eternal life: and they are they which testify of me.

Romans 5:21

[21] That as sin hath reigned unto death, even so might grace reign through righteousness unto eternal life by Jesus Christ our Lord.

Galatians 6:8

8 For he that soweth to his flesh shall of the flesh reap cor-
ruption; but he that soweth to the Spirit shall of the Spirit
reap life everlasting.

Paul refers to 'eternal life' as the result of a committed life of righteousness. John emphasizes 'eternal life' as the present reality and possession of the Christian who *believes*!

Eternal life is a person's new and redeemed existence in Jesus Christ
that is granted by God as a gift to all believers.

Eternal life refers to the quality or character of that new life. Although
all persons will live through eternity, not all will have a pleasant experience. The sinner in eternity will be enduring torment, shame, and pain
in hell which will be cast into the lake of fire. But the Christian in eternity
will have a life of joyful peace and rest in the presence of the Lord Jesus
Christ.

Now, we can see why one condition is described as everlasting life
and the other as everlasting torment, because life in eternity is something
to be enjoyed, not endured in torment.

The sad fact is that most people live for the present moment and
ignore the consequences awaiting them at the end of life. In fact, most
people live in a manner that ignores the consequences awaiting them
right here and now. We eat and drink and have a lifestyle that will lead to
certain sicknesses and disease, but we turn a blind eye and say, "Let me
enjoy it for the moment." When the time comes to pay for the error of our
ways we always want a quick way out, but what has taken years to build
up is hard to get rid of in a moment.

So we see people all around us suffering the consequences of their erroneous choices on a daily basis. But what makes it even more regretful is that others do not learn from their mistakes; they go right ahead a follow that same path to destruction.

Jesus made it clear that 'eternal life' comes only to those who make a total commitment to Him. Have you?

> *I declare that I will try with the help of the Lord to live a life of fulfillment and purpose with the attendant joys available in this life, the most important of which is preparation for Eternal Life in Christ for eternity.*
>
> *I will do all in my power to reveal these truths to others.*

Family, Motherhood

Since human times began, our core community and sustenance in good times and bad has always been our family, and the clan deriving from those blood relationships.

Our relationship with family is important, as that is usually where we learn our values, our behaviors, and our place in life and in the world. That is where we return when things don't go well for us out in the world.

If things are not going well in our relationship with family members, things are not going well at all in any aspect of our life. At least, that has been my observation!

We each have multiple daily opportunities to improve and greatly develop the love and support for our family members, as these are the individuals that we spend most of our time with. With the guidance of Jesus Christ, our Bible and our Christian community, it is possible to create a loving and supportive relationship with family – that can then naturally extend to all the other people in your life.

Family

2 Corinthians 5:18

And all things are of God, who hath reconciled us to himself by Jesus Christ, and hath given to us the ministry of reconciliation.

1 John 5:7

For there are three that bear record in heaven, the Father, the Word, and the Holy Ghost: and these three are one.

What are we? Are we some abstract life form placed here to endure continual pains and intermittent triumphs? Is there a goal to our existence? Why am I here? What is my purpose?

These are a few of the vexing queries many people have as they interact with life, and there are no reasonable soul-satisfying answers in sight.

The answer can be found in modeling the original family relationship. The Bible makes it clear that the Father, Son and Holy Spirit work in perfect unison.

We can reconcile ourselves to God through Jesus Christ and become part of the great Family of God. The excellent truth is that we experience the deep inner peace which takes away the frustrating quest for temporal answers about our existence.

In addition, God has also given us an earthly personal family, and although the individuals possess varying characteristics, our tie to the Family of God is intended to positively influence our earthly family.

The deep sense of satisfaction that comes from the fellowship of our earthly family cannot be replaced. It is therefore required of us to do what is made clear in the scripture of Corinthians above, and enjoy the family plan of God. If you have a fragmented family, reach out to God and He will empower you to reach out in the ministry of reconciliation to your family.

> *I declare* that every trap of the enemy – for my life, spouse, family, home, church, workplace, children, grandchildren, aunts, uncles, cousins, in-laws – that each trap be revealed and brought to nothing.

> *I declare* that this same group will do what is necessary for reconciliation and to inherit eternal life in Christ.

Mother's Bond

II Kings 4:12-23

12 And he said to Gehazi his servant, Call this Shunammite. And when he had called her, she stood before him.

13 And he said unto him, Say now unto her, Behold, thou hast been careful for us with all this care; what is to be done for thee? Wouldest thou be spoken for to the king, or to the captain of the host? And she answered, I dwell among mine own people.

14 And he said, What then is to be done for her? And Gehazi answered, Verily she hath no child, and her husband is old.

15 And he said, Call her. And when he had called her, she stood in the door.

16 And he said, About this season, according to the time of life, thou shalt embrace a son. And she said, Nay, my lord, thou man of God, do not lie unto thine handmaid.

17 And the woman conceived, and bare a son at that season that Elisha had said unto her, according to the time of life.

18 And when the child was grown, it fell on a day, that he went out to his father to the reapers.

19 And he said unto his father, My head, my head. And he said to a lad, Carry him to his mother.

20 And when he had taken him, and brought him to his mother, he sat on her knees till noon, and then died.

21 And she went up, and laid him on the bed of the man of God, and shut the door upon him, and went out.

22 And she called unto her husband, and said, Send me, I pray thee, one of the young men, and one of the asses, that I may run to the man of God, and come again.

23 And he said, Wherefore wilt thou go to him today? It is neither new moon, nor Sabbath. And she said, It shall be well.

First of all, I want you to notice that the Shunammite woman was displaying motherly qualities in her care for Elisha before she actually became a mother. The second thing I want you to notice is that she did not have any hesitation when it came to putting Faith to work when her son died; she declared, "It shall be well". She immediately knew and took action (demonstrated her faith with works) to reach the only source that could help her in this situation. The third thing that I want you to notice is that she kept a single-minded focus, and called the thing that had not yet materialized as if it already had been done, by her constant confession of "It shall be well".

Today we will look at the bond between a Mother and a child that is so well exemplified in this Bible account. That bond has something that cannot quite be explained in words. Those of us who come into contact with that bond are often left at a loss for words, because it just cannot be explained why a mother would go to such lengths, with a single-minded focus to revive what appears to everyone else a dead (hopeless) condition concerning her child.

This lady was careful to avoid any negatives being spoken to her, she was not going to allow anyone or anything to deter her from this walk of Faith and determination, and so she simply said to her husband, "It shall be well". These words were not just an answer; they were the affirmation of her faith. These were not just simply words; they were a declaration of victory before the battle was over. These words were the manifestation of the bond that exists between a mother and a child.

Jesus our Lord wants to prove this same type of Love Bond to you in your life. He will go all the way for you, even when everyone thinks that you are hopeless and have written you off as dead.

> *I declare that the banner of the Love of the Lord is over me! His deep care undergirds me, His Blood protects me, His Word guides me, His Peace keeps me. I'm resting in the assurance of His Love.*

Temptation and Sin, Abiding in the Lord

The Bible refers to 'temptation' and 'sin' well over 1,000 times. That gives us a strong clue that we need to pay attention to this aspect of how we live in the world, and to how we live in our hearts!

As humans, we tend to rationalize temptation, sin, and how we cave in to them... or how we really don't.

As we read our Bible for guidance on how to deal with this very human issue, we understand that even an unspoken thought deviating from Jesus Christ's guidance is a sin. We come to understand that a sinful thought, even if we never act on it, is still a sin.

Eventually, we realize that sin begins with our thoughts and feelings, and turn to Christ the Lord for guidance in purifying and redirecting those thoughts. Abiding in Him, turning to Him to cleanse us – these may be new habits. But with Him, all is possible.

The Bottleneck

Galatians 5:22-23
[22] *But the fruit of the Spirit is love, joy, peace, longsuffering, gentleness, goodness, faith,*
[23] *meekness, temperance: against such there is no law.*

Did you ever notice that no matter when you begin your journey (mostly by automobile), the timing seems to be just right for you to meet another vehicle/person at the most narrow portion of the pathway? This can be the roadway, a narrow bridge or some other impediment or situation which requires some adjustment on your or the other individual's part. This 'bottleneck' can be one of the most frustrating experiences if not appreciated for what it actually is. Well then, what is it?

I'm glad you asked! It is a test of our resolve, patience, self-control, humility, willingness to put others and the greater good above oneself. It is not an opportunity to try out all those colorful gestures and ungodly epithets that are best kept on the back streets of nowhere! Do not cave in to the temptation! This is a chance to step into the shoes of Christ in His infinite love and compassion.

The proof of what Christ has birthed in us is of no use unless it can be demonstrated in a practical and applicable manner to a world where impatience, anger and every evil temptation is pervasive. Our Christ-like response to life's bottlenecks may just be the tool which draws some distraught soul to Him.

Therefore, let us renew our minds and look at the bottleneck situations as opportunities to demonstrate Christ, rather than sources of frustration. Smile: He chose *you* to demonstrate His Love.

I decide today to let the "fruit of the Spirit" be my guiding principle. I realize that this will take practice and a consistent attitude, but with the Lord's help, *I declare* it is achievable.

I rejoice in the opportunity to demonstrate His Love!

Yield Not to Temptation

I Corinthians 10:13

¹³ *There hath no temptation taken you but such as is common to man: but God is faithful, who will not suffer you to be tempted above that ye are able; but will with the temptation also make a way to escape, that ye may be able to bear it.*

Let us take a moment of silence and think on the weight of those words of scripture...

The fact of the matter is that we will be overtaken by various sorts of temptations. There is no escaping that. Although the temptations will vary from person to person, we all have our areas of weakness in which we are tested or tempted.

The Word points out that in all of these temptations the one thing is that they are common or normal occurrences for mankind. The next statement is one of great encouragement, 'but God is faithful.' Oh, thank God for His faithfulness! You see, we need a faithful God in the midst of a troubled and temptation-filled life. His faithfulness is what sustains us when we stumble and fall as we often do, whether our pride will allow us to admit it or not, but remember our reading about 'him that who thinketh he standeth take heed, lest he fall'. You see, pride comes to open the door to our destruction and downfall, so if we resist pride we will avoid downfall. The temptation to walk in our pride is a temptation to build on false and faulty foundations. We all know that the strength of a building is in its foundation, just as the strength of our life is in the spiritual foundations we lay. Let us lay it on the Rock of Christ Jesus and not on our false sense of pride.

As we go along, we see that our scripture tells us that the temptation is controlled by God the faithful one, who will not allow it to be more than we can bear. It is always just enough to produce the results that God is looking for from us, if we endure the temptation without succumbing to it. You see, we will be stronger for the experience if we overcome the temptation, but we will be weaker if we yield to the temptation, the decision is entirely up to us and our level of trust and faith in God.

> *I declare* that I will cast down imaginations and every high thing that exalts itself against the knowledge of God, and bring every thought captive to the obedience of Christ.

> *I agree* to bind those things that hinder my spiritual life and loose those things that promote my spiritual wellness, knowing that whatever I bind and loose on earth is bound and loosed in Heaven.

Harden Not Your Heart

Exodus 17:2-7

² Wherefore the people did chide with Moses, and said, Give us water that we may drink. And Moses said unto them, Why chide ye with me? Wherefore do ye tempt the LORD?

³ And the people thirsted there for water; and the people murmured against Moses, and said, Wherefore is this that thou hast brought us up out of Egypt, to kill us and our children and our cattle with thirst?

⁴ And Moses cried unto the LORD, saying, What shall I do unto this people? They be almost ready to stone me.

⁵ And the LORD said unto Moses, Go on before the people, and take with thee of the elders of Israel; and thy rod, wherewith thou smotest the river, take in thine hand, and go.

⁶ Behold, I will stand before thee there upon the rock in Horeb; and thou shalt smite the rock, and there shall come water out of it, that the people may drink. And Moses did so in the sight of the elders of Israel.

⁷ And he called the name of the place Massah, and Meribah, because of the chiding of the children of Israel, and because they tempted the LORD, saying, Is the LORD among us, or not?

Psalm 95:7-8

⁷ For he is our God; and we are the people of his pasture, and the sheep of his hand. To day if ye will hear his voice,

⁸ Harden not your heart, as in the provocation, and as in the day of temptation in the wilderness:

The human spirit is very fickle. By that I mean we are so often and so easily turned aside and we give up hope – in spite of the fact that we have had so many experiences of victory and successes.

It seems that with each new challenge, we go back to the bottom of a hopeless pit although we were just on the mountaintop! This is a crucial point for all leaders to be aware of, that no matter how great the success of the most recent victory, the people have a great propensity to only remember the negatives or failures. They do not build their hopes and encourage themselves by the positives gained and learned from the most recent victory.

It is in this type of mindset and the resultant *attitudes* that Moses finds himself as he tries through the help and obedience to God to get a people (Israel) from bondage to true freedom and the Promised Land. Now, Moses was not dwelling on the things of Egypt for they were in the past, but the people always used the past bondage and its experiences as their reference point in facing the **present conditions,** which were only a vehicle to their future success.

I want all leaders as well as the people who follow them to know that your **present condition** is only a vehicle to get you to where God ultimately has prepared for you to be and enjoy. Just like the people of Israel lost sight of the big picture on their way from bondage to the Promised Land of freedom, today people lose sight of the big picture in life.

We have to learn to raise our spiritual insight above what we see presently and realize that in the larger scheme of things, this is just another milestone towards the end. Now, this is very important, because if the people see it, then they will have a "let's get through this" mentality instead of a "let's blame the leader and complain" mentality. This being the case, the leader can then concentrate on the next step towards freedom instead of having to re-teach over and over that the things of the past must remain in the past because we are going somewhere better. This distraction of having to deal with past issues is what causes us to go in circles instead of making progress in the direction of freedom, victory and the Promised Land. These values hold true whether in religious or secular circles, because we all deal with the same type of mannerisms.

But today, if the people of God will do as the Psalmist encourages us, we will take the lead in showing the rest of the world how to enjoy true victory and success – regardless of the bad experiences of the past.

*Today as I hear His Voice, **I decide** not to harden my heart.*

***I declare** a mantle of forward thinking to cover me and my leadership in all areas of life.*

***I declare** that the past will no longer hold my future hostage; rather the chains of the past are broken now as we advance to the freedom which Christ has made for us.*

The Transgressor

Galatians 2:18
For if I build again the things which I destroyed, I make myself a transgressor.

Life is full of successes and failures, indeed our failures are more numerous than our successes. It is from the numerous failures that the few successes become so sweet and cherished. Because of our make-up, humans are simply more prone to failures; what I mean is that we have to struggle so hard to have a success in any venture, but failure seems to take absolutely no effort at all to achieve! And so we live a life tempered by our many failures and few successes.

This is the great test of life, for those whom we call the strong are actually those who have been able to hold on to the positives of their successes and build on them with more hope and faith. And those whom we call the weak are those who concentrate on their (and others') many failures and lose faith and hope in the defeatist mentality.

Do you see that the successes come when we are able to destroy those things that cause us to fail so often? Whatever the cause may be – sometimes it is a certain relationship, a bad habit, a certain weakness or a source of temptation that needs to be destroyed – until its destruction, we will not see success.

So now our text says to us, *'For if I build again the things which I destroyed, I make myself a transgressor.'* Apostle Paul is making a very valid point for continued success. Since successes are so few, the great tragedy of life is going back to that which we have already conquered. After having finally tasted the sweetness of victory, do we allow the old temptation to build up in us to the point where we fall back into the failure lifestyle concerning that particular thing? You see when you go back, you make yourself a transgressor – you break the law of good, grace, and success for the emptiness that comes with failures.

But the reason often times is because of our humanity. We still want to go back to that which is most comfortable to us, even if it is a lifestyle of failure, because the area of success and victory is strange territory! We often do not trust it or know how to handle success and victory, as so we become transgressors, and it is a great tragedy of life when this happens.

But, there is hope for the transgressor. There is still new life awaiting those who have been overcome by the many failures in life. There is strength and peace awaiting you and it is all found in Jesus Christ. For you see, where we are weak, He is strong. His strength is made perfect in our weaknesses. To win this battle of Life we need a strong friend and His name is Jesus.

> *I declare* *that "Many are the afflictions of the righteous: but the LORD delivereth him out of them all," and I will continuously be delivered because of His promise.*

> *I decide* *to retain my successes and look at my failures only as experience gained but not to be revisited.*

> *I declare* *that goodness and mercy shall follow me all the days of my life.*

Face and Voice of the Lord

Throughout spiritual history, individual believers have declared that they have seen the face of God or heard the voice of the Lord. I personally believe that we all are capable of having such experiences!

Jesus Christ comes to us directly, with no intermediary required. He comes to us directly when we have no apparent pressing need, but are quiet in our hearts and minds. He indeed comes to us with direct guidance and words of solace, in moments of great need when we solicit his guidance or ask to hear his voice.

Christ our Lord is ever-present. Listen. Watch quietly. He is ever with you.

Who's On Your Side? (Separate Me)

Romans 8:31
What shall we then say to these things? If God be for us, who can be against us?

Romans 8:35
Who shall separate us from the love of Christ? Shall trib-ulation, or distress, or persecution, or famine, or naked-ness, or peril, or sword?

There are a lot of questions being asked, and there seems to be an at-mosphere of complacency, resignation and acceptance of a fate that we know in our hearts that God did not intend for us to have. A fate of oppression, defeat, unfulfilled dreams, messed up opportunities, under-achievement separate us from the voice of the Lord. Broken lives, rela-tionships, families and a broken society are all being accepted as normal and something to be tolerated as God's will and way. Have we not simply stopped hearing the Lord's voice? Have we not simply stopped looking into the Lord's eyes, even as we ask for His guidance?

Under the guise of compromise and shirking responsibility, we say, "See what they did?" The need to embrace every false doctrine is strong, in an effort not to offend anyone, but to please everyone. And this really satisfies no one.

Quite an impossible task and a very great delusion, but this seems to be the trend of trying to be accepted and to avoid the sting of rejection which comes by standing for the *real* Truth. It has never been so bad as it is now, where those who claim to have the truth of Christ are busy trying to be accepted by those of false doctrines and false religions!

It is time for someone to stand and say that the One and Only way to God is through Jesus Christ, the only salvation for the sinful human soul is by the *blood of Jesus* and His precious Grace. There is absolutely no other way. To entertain any other doctrine is simply a waste of time, an exercise in futility and a trick of the enemy to keep us busy with falsehood and to eventually miss the mark.

This business of doing good, and pleasing those who do not want to be told that they are wrong is going to lead more people to hell than anything else. I submit to you that it is wrapped up in the fear of loss of relationship with man, and hoping that God will understand. But we must take the position of the Apostle Paul in **Romans 8:35** and say *"Who shall separate us from the love of Christ? Shall tribulation, or nakedness, or peril, or sword?"* We must place our relationship and our stand for Christ above all else, for we do not know how long we have on earth to do what we *must* do for Christ.

The time to hear the voice of God is now, the opportunity to stand for truth and Christ is now. The time is now – for who shall separate me from the love of Christ? If God be for me, who can be against me?

The amazing thing about people is this. Whenever someone dies, the first question is "Were they right with God?" Yet we continue to live contrary to the Word of God, everyone is so concerned about being right with God *after* someone dies. It is a great trick of the enemy! We need to get right with God NOW! The time is now!

Look upon His face and heed His voice, and then continue to live without the fear of death. Do not be fooled my dear readers, the concern of eternity is to take care of your soul's salvation now, not run around after death and ask the question.

Stop being afraid of man whom you see for a brief moment, and stand for Christ and His truth which is eternal.

> *I declare* that the fear of man will no longer hold me hostage! I will only reverence and fear God who is able to destroy both body and soul in hell, and not man who can only kill the body.

> *I declare* that this is the day that the Lord has made. *I will rejoice* and be glad in it, because I know that God is for me and therefore it does not matter who is against me.

The Voice of the Lord

Luke 1:26-38

[26] *And in the sixth month the angel Gabriel was sent from God unto a city of Galilee, named Nazareth,*

[27] *To a virgin espoused to a man whose name was Joseph, of the house of David; and the virgin's name was Mary.*

[28] *And the angel came in unto her, and said, Hail, thou that art highly favoured, the Lord is with thee: blessed art thou among women.*

[29] *And when she saw him, she was troubled at his saying, and cast in her mind what manner of salutation this should be.*

[30] *And the angel said unto her, Fear not, Mary: for thou hast found favour with God.*

[31] *And, behold, thou shalt conceive in thy womb, and bring forth a son, and shalt call his name Jesus.*

[32] *He shall be great, and shall be called the Son of the Highest: and the Lord God shall give unto him the throne of his father David:*

[33] *And he shall reign over the house of Jacob for ever; and of his kingdom there shall be no end.*

[34] *Then said Mary unto the angel, How shall this be, seeing I know not a man?*

[35] *And the angel answered and said unto her, The Holy Ghost shall come upon thee, and the power of the Highest shall overshadow thee: therefore also that holy thing which shall be born of thee shall be called the Son of God.*

[36] *And, behold, thy cousin Elisabeth, she hath also conceived a son in her old age: and this is the sixth month with her, who was called barren.*

[37] *For with God nothing shall be impossible.*

38 And Mary said, Behold the handmaid of the Lord; be it unto me according to thy word. And the angel departed from her.

The desire of everyone's heart whether they know it, realize it or admit it is that they hear from the Lord for themselves. Not necessarily to see the face of God with our eyes, but to hear His voice directed to our ears as we try to figure out our way through life.

Now, hearing from the Lord is not like hearing from people, because when you hear from the Lord it changes your outlook on life and more importantly, you _must_ do according to what you heard the Lord say!

The challenge or quandary comes when what "thus saith the Lord" to you is in opposition or outside of 'normal' thinking or reasoning to you and everyone else on earth. Alas, it often seems so! But pause and ponder before ignoring the Wisdom given to you. For Wisdom it is…

And so we are a human race desiring to hear from the Lord for ourselves, but we are essentially unprepared to trust the Lord through obedience to what He said. This is because we are receiving spiritual information or instructions and processing it through our carnal or natural way of living.

Understanding this, we can then begin to appreciate the dilemma that Mary found herself in when the Angel of the Lord gave her what was at that time the most shocking news not only for her life but indeed through all the ages. Can you imagine being told you will conceive a child without having done what every human must do to have a child, and added to that, this child will be the Son of God? My dear readers, hearing from God is simply not a regular experience, and to receive what is heard takes even more faith that ever imagined before! But if we take the example of

Mary receiving the Word with gladness and obedience and act on it, we will be the better for the experience.

We are all blessed because of Mary's obedience. Maybe the blessing of someone is depending on your obedience to the Word of the Lord, for when God speaks He speaks not only into our present, but also into our future. He speaks blessings, healing, deliverance, hope, joy and peace all in the same utterance. The volumes of what was said to Mary is still being unfolded until now and we still have not gotten our hands – let alone our minds – around it, and indeed, we may never! That is just how great God is.

So when He speaks, we must listen and obey, for it will benefit not only us, but all who hear and come into contact with us and future generations. The benefits and blessings of the Lord are tied up in obedience: Will you start down that road of obedience today? Mary did, and we are still walking in it. Will you begin for your generations today to walk with the Lord in obedience?

> Father **I thank you** for this day of Grace. Even though my mind may wander, you bring me back to your fold. You are the great shepherd and **I am grateful** to listen and hear your voice as it leads me gently along life's pathway.
>
> **I realize** that your thoughts and ways are higher than mine and are past my finding out, so **I declare** that I will be obedient to your voice now and forever.

Truth and Falsehood

Truth and falsehood have brought great nations to take up arms against each other. One is declaring that they have the great, unblemished truth, and that the other is spewing falsehoods – and vice versa. We see this as well between two individuals, pitted against each other for whatever excuse or reason.

Truth. Falsehood. The distinction sometimes brings strong men to their knees.

The core attribute of all truth is often hard for rationalizing mankind to accept, and it is this: *Truth is always expressed quietly, in few words, with great simplicity.*

Because of this core attribute of simplicity, we are often tested in our faith and belief when Jesus Christ expresses the simple truth to us about any situation, circumstance or ourselves. It is our job, as it were, to sit as quietly of heart and mind as we can when the Lord Jesus speaks His truth to us. Push your ego out of the equation. Let go of worldly assumptions and the convoluted rationalizations of the ordinary mind.

Without Me

John 1:2-4

²The same was in the beginning with God.
³All things were made by him; and without him was not any thing made that was made.
⁴In him was life; and the life was the light of men.

John 15:4-5

⁴Abide in me, and I in you. As the branch cannot bear fruit of itself, except it abide in the vine; no more can ye, except ye abide in me.
⁵I am the vine, ye are the branches: He that abideth in me, and I in him, the same bringeth forth much fruit: for without me ye can do nothing.

James 4:13-15

¹³Go to now, ye that say, Today or tomorrow we will go into such a city, and continue there a year, and buy and sell, and get gain:
¹⁴Whereas ye know not what shall be on the morrow. For what is your life? It is even a vapour, that appeareth for a little time, and then vanisheth away.
¹⁵For that ye ought to say, If the Lord will, we shall live, and do this, or that.

There are many thoughts that flood the mind when the seriousness of the declaration by Jesus "without me you can do nothing" hits home. I will mention three such things.

Our *humanity* should be one such thought, although we think we are the sustainers of our lives, the truth is that we are nothing without the 'Self Existent One'.

Our *abilities* also spring to mind, how often we take for granted the natural gifts we have, and the acquired skills we develop as products of our making. Truth be told, we are nothing except what Christ has given us and allowed us to be. The Word of God declares that without Him nothing that is made was made.

Our *future* is what I believe to be the number one factor in life which we take for granted, as if it were guaranteed or owed to us in some way.

But the truth of the Word brings it into perspective when we reread James 4:13-15 (above). Abide in this moment you have been given.

*I **declare** that in Jesus I live and move and have my being.*

*I **recognize** that without Him, I am and can do nothing. That is why **I submit** by thoughts, plans and wishes to His control.*

Too Late

II Corinthians 4: 3-4

³ But if our gospel be hid, it is hid to them that are lost:
⁴ In whom the god of this world hath blinded the minds of them which believe not, lest the light of the glorious gospel of Christ, who is the image of God, should shine unto them.

The story most often told by people's lives is that we only want to hear about Jesus after we die. Can you imagine that? After we die!

Now, this is not said in plain words, but can be read by the actions (or lack thereof) that people portray not just today, but for a very long time. Even think back on Barabbas, the criminal who was chosen by the people over Jesus at Pilate's judgment hall. Now, we are all glad that Jesus was not chosen to escape death, for where would we be today without Jesus' sacrifice?

But the question is, *why does nobody want to hear about Jesus?* You see the reason is that this world has blinded people and would have you believe that loving Jesus, having your sins forgiven by Jesus, is a bad thing, a crazy experience and not a reasonable way to live.

That is a lie. A big part of that lie is that the only time you need Jesus is to make it to heaven, and so therefore only worry about Him *when death comes along for you*. But who ever knows when death is coming along for them? So we have people with the mindset of "I will instruct my family to call the preacher when I'm on my deathbed" or "I will look for Jesus in the grave or shortly before the grave."

We who are not blinded by this know that such a time is just too late. The truth is that the time for Jesus is now.

I declare that I will no longer deceive myself with a "later for Jesus" mentality. *I will take* the positive step of believing in my heart the Lord Jesus Christ, and confessing with my mouth my need of forgiveness and His salvation.

Truth vs False Knowledge

Acts 4:10-12

[10] Be it known unto you all, and to all the people of Israel, that by the name of Jesus Christ of Nazareth, whom ye crucified, whom God raised from the dead, even by him doth this man stand here before you whole.

[11] This is the stone which was set at nought of you builders, which is become the head of the corner.

[12] Neither is there salvation in any other: for there is none other name under heaven given among men, whereby we must be saved.

There is so much information spreading throughout the world today, the intention of which is to confuse the minds of people so that they do not take the required action to save their souls.

Now, knowledge is good, yes indeed! However, in our knowing we must come to a knowledge of the *truth*. It is truth which will make us free. This is very important, for to always be learning, yet never coming to the knowledge of the *truth* is an exercise in futility.

Well you may ask, what then is the truth? *Truth is a fact that proves itself by actually doing or producing what it said it will do or produce.* With truth, a secondary witness or confirmation is not needed to prove itself to be genuine. This is why when we receive salvation in the name of Jesus, we have the witness within ourselves by the Spirit of God, and we testify of our own accord, "My life has been changed – Hallelujah!" We do not need someone to tell us or a council to deliberate and consider the facts. We are our own proof of the Truth of the words of the Bible, that is truth in action, proving on its own that what it said will be, actually comes to be.

This is the dividing line between Bible Truth and other forms of knowledge.

We hear a lot today about all forms of knowledge (science, history and so on). But when it comes to real change occurring in men's lives, when it comes to a personal proof of making the difference to a lifestyle of sin and shame and defeat – well, these other forms of knowledge do not and cannot show a proof of effectiveness. They don't ever measure up to what salvation in the name of Jesus does for a man.

When you really check them out, they surround themselves with a lot of fancy words but still practice what is sinful and binding to the soul. They use a lot of ordinary-mind logic, but produce no real change in the heart.

My readers, the *heart* has to be changed, or it will only be a pretense for a while. Do not be fooled. God is not mocked, and whatsoever a man sows, that shall he also reap. No semblance of knowledge is going to have God change His requirements for access to eternal life in His presence. It is only by the door of Jesus Christ that you can be saved and can be in the right place for eternity. All other arguments will mean absolutely *nothing* when you stand before God to give an account for the decisions you made in life.

I say again, knowledge is good, however the most important knowledge is to know the Lord Jesus Christ in the personal pardoning of your sins.

Let this Truth of our scripture from Acts abide with you – there is salvation in no other but Jesus the Christ. This had proven itself countless times in the lives of many millions. Do not be lost in worldly knowledge or seek salvation in it – it will not save you. Come instead to the saving knowledge of Jesus Christ the Lord.

I have decided to make Jesus my choice. As knowledge in the world increases, the simple truth of salvation by Jesus Christ remains the same.

I am willing to accept the testimony of millions and the Word of God that Jesus is the Way, the Truth and the Life, and no one comes to the Father except by Him.

Failure and Success

In our modern societies, we seem to be obsessed with attaining worldly success. Failure embarrasses us… We are like ostriches with our head in the sand, in denial that we were ever capable of failure.

On the other hand, success goes to our heads. We lose sight, perhaps, of our core values in Christ, as we focus on material success, worldly fame, or on our increasing financial wealth.

It is far too easy to lose sight of the real fact that failure is one of our best teachers! Failure brings opportunities to learn, grow and become more effective in Christ and in His world. It is far too easy to lose sight of the real fact that your material world wealth and success can be brought to the altar of Christ to further His mission and His purposes.

Success is not the same as inner happiness or inner peace! The source of your talent, abilities, opportunities – and thus your success in the world – is the Lord! Remembering this will increase your success, in perfect balance with your own inner happiness and inner peace.

What Type of Mind Do You Have?

Philippians 2:5
Let this mind be in you, which was also in Christ Jesus

Philippians 4:7
And the peace of God, which passeth all understanding, shall keep your hearts and minds through Christ Jesus.

This will take some thought, for the question being asked today is, "What do you think about how you think?"

We are saying that we should stop and consider how our thought patterns work for or against us. How we deal with situations and things we encounter in life starts with our thought(s) about them, right? Do we think of a just and peaceful solution to things, or do we react (think) in an aggressive and undignified manner?   In short, how do we think?

Why is this important?

If you, for instance, have a situation that could best be settled by exercising a little patience, but your thought incorrectly led you to react in an aggressive manner – then what could have been a smooth resolution instead becomes an uncomfortable situation. Just because of the way you think about it!

Now, that is something to reflect on. How often in our lifetime have we seen potentially good situations go sour just because somebody acted upon a wrong thought? That wrong idea came because we often times think ill, when we should exercise patience and think positively.

Go again to *Philippians*. We have to make a conscious effort to begin to let our mind think along the lines of Jesus' thinking. Jesus – when He was reviled, when he was slapped and spit upon – did not retaliate. I am not saying to lay down and take whatever happens to you. I am saying that our mindset, our way of thinking, should *first* take the path that peace is possible and the best resolution for all involved. It is in no one's best interest to always have our tempers flaring and voices shouting, while nothing positive is actually being achieved. There is a time and place for everything, and when we take time to let our mind flow along the lines of the mind of the Lord Jesus Christ we can only be better off for the experience.

Jesus also instructed us to forgive as often as necessary each day, to do good, to love, to bless and to pray for our enemies. Now, that is the type of mindset – a kind of thought pattern – that we must make an effort to acquire! For when we move to this type of thinking, a lot of life's problems will disappear. We are so accustomed to holding bitterness and envy in our hearts, that we find is extremely difficult to think as Jesus instructed us to think ... or to go even further and actually act like Jesus instructed us to act. As I said earlier, this will take some active reflection, and if we think this out prayerfully, we will all come to the conclusion that in all things, especially our thoughts, Jesus is the answer for the world today.

> *I declare that I will let this mind be in me which was also in Christ Jesus, who when he was reviled did not retaliate in kind. With the Lord as my helper, I will try to be mature in my interactions and not emotional in my responses.*

What Did You Agree Upon?

Matthew 20:1-2

¹For the kingdom of heaven is like unto a man that is a householder, which went out early in the morning to hire labourers into his vineyard.

² And when he had agreed with the labourers for a penny a day, he sent them into his vineyard.

³ And he went out about the third hour, and saw others standing idle in the marketplace,

⁴ And said unto them; Go ye also into the vineyard, and whatsoever is right I will give you. And they went their way.

⁵ Again he went out about the sixth and ninth hour, and did likewise.

⁶ And about the eleventh hour he went out, and found others standing idle, and saith unto them, Why stand ye here all the day idle?

⁷ They say unto him, Because no man hath hired us. He saith unto them, Go ye also into the vineyard; and whatsoever is right, that shall ye receive.

⁸ So when even was come, the lord of the vineyard saith unto his steward, Call the labourers, and give them their hire, beginning from the last unto the first.

⁹ And when they came that were hired about the eleventh hour, they received every man a penny.

¹⁰ But when the first came, they supposed that they should have received more; and they likewise received every man a penny.

¹¹ And when they had received it, they murmured against the good man of the house,

¹² Saying, These last have wrought but one hour, and thou hast made them equal unto us, which have borne the burden and heat of the day.

13 But he answered one of them, and said, Friend, I do thee no wrong: didst not thou agree with me for a penny?

14 Take that thine is, and go thy way: I will give unto this last, even as unto thee.

15 Is it not lawful for me to do what I will with mine own? Is thine eye evil, because I am good?

16 So the last shall be first, and the first last: for many be called, but few chosen.

Here we are speaking of ethics and morality. We are speaking of being a "man of your word."

You may feel that life or other individuals have failed you. That life has been unfair to you or that others have not lived up to their agreements with you. But is that so? Have you misinterpreted the agreement in the first place? Have you agreed to terms that you did not pay attention to – or did you agree nonchalantly, just to get things over with, so that you could move on? There are also, alas, those who believe that no matter what the agreement is, they are not really bound to its terms, or that they can change the terms at any time if they so choose.

Be honest with yourself. Be honest with others. What did you agree to? Why?

The best of business people nowadays say, "Everything is negotiable" and, in a very real sense, that is so. But what were the terms that you would have needed in order to say, "I can live with this" ... in order to say, "I can follow through on this."

What did you agree upon with these others? With your employer, are you complaining of work conditions and wages? With your spouse, are you not happy with the marriage vows you made? Are you disappointed in your child's behavior, thinking they are not obeying House Rules? With the Lord, are you jealous that someone else is being blessed 'more' than you seem to be?

God will call people into this glorious gospel right down to the last minute – but is that a reason for you to lose your years in the Lord?

The Bible tells us that the first shall be last and last shall be first. A spirit of selfishness will cause us to want more than the agreed amount. What is it that you have agreed to?

> *I declare that I will be a person of 'my word', knowing that to betray my character values for material gain is actually a loss.*
>
> *I trust that others will see my honesty and I truly believe that I will reap the rewards of faithfulness to my agreements.*

Reality

Philippians 4:13
I can do all things through Christ which strengtheneth me.

Now if we take this look at this verse of scripture, the scoffer or the opponent of truth will say, "How can I possibly do all things? Can I be a fireman, doctor, lawyer, policeman, cook and teacher all in one lifetime? Can I do everything necessary to make it through life on my own?"

If we take that attitude, we are denying the gist of the Word, for *'all things'* here does not refer to being a Jack of all trades. Rather it refers to our ability to accomplish *all that is necessary* to fulfill our <u>own</u> purpose and our <u>own</u> calling.

So then, if in the pursuit of our purpose and calling in life we meet an obstacle, we can speak this word to it. We say, "I am called to do this, and since you are blocking my path or are a hindrance to my completion, I want to let you know that *I can do all things necessary to complete my calling, because of Christ who strengthens me!*"

You may ask, "Preacher, how does He strengthen me?" He strengthens not as we count strength in a physical manner (although He gives that, too) but in this context, He strengthens by giving us the ability to think of solutions ... by giving us the Peace to keep our sanity in the situation ... by opening doors of opportunity ... by giving favour in places where without Him it would have been impossible ... by making our enemies to be at peace with us ... by working things out simply by Faith in Him.

Strength, in other words, takes on many forms!

In all of these ways and more, the Lord Jesus Christ strengthens us for the tasks we are given in life. So as you face your task, whatever may come along in your efforts to accomplish and complete that task, let yourself be edified and strengthened by knowledge of the fact that in Christ Jesus you have the ability to do all things that are your purpose and calling.

Please take note that the key factor is _in Christ Jesus_, and if you are not in Christ Jesus this simply does not apply to you! So hurry to get in Christ Jesus! You see the Bible has a lot of promises and assurances, but they hinge on having a relationship with the Lord. Now, relationship with the Lord is free for the asking and sweet in the receiving.

Now my question to you is, "What is your purpose and calling in life? What has been hindering you from fulfilling that purpose?" Is it fear of ridicule, of being judged and talked about? Is it fear of your own inability to get the job done? Is it a lack of knowledge of financial things or management? Is it simply laziness and a lack of drive and determination? Is it a family crisis? Is it peer pressure?

All these things and more hinder us from doing what we are called to do in life. Whatever it is, speak this word to it, _"I can do all things through Christ which strengtheneth me"_ and move on in Faith.

> _**I remember**_ _I must be in Jesus Christ, for in Him I truly can do all things. This is the Reality of Life._

> _**I declare**_ _that I will fulfill my purpose and complete my destiny which God has ordained before I was born._

> _**I will align myself**_ _with the will of God, recognizing that His strength is all I need to succeed._

Do Not Be Afraid To Fail

Joshua 1: 1-9

1 Now after the death of Moses the servant of the Lord it came to pass, that the Lord spake unto Joshua the son of Nun, Moses' minister, saying,

2 Moses my servant is dead; now therefore arise, go over this Jordan, thou, and all this people, unto the land which I do give to them, even to the children of Israel.

3 Every place that the sole of your foot shall tread upon, that have I given unto you, as I said unto Moses.

4 From the wilderness and this Lebanon even unto the great river, the river Euphrates, all the land of the Hittites, and unto the great sea toward the going down of the sun, shall be your coast.

5 There shall not any man be able to stand before thee all the days of thy life: as I was with Moses, so I will be with thee: I will not fail thee, nor forsake thee.

6 Be strong and of a good courage: for unto this people shalt thou divide for an inheritance the land, which I sware unto their fathers to give them.

7 Only be thou strong and very courageous, that thou mayest observe to do according to all the law, which Moses my servant commanded thee: turn not from it to the right hand or to the left, that thou mayest prosper withersoever thou goest.

8 This book of the law shall not depart out of thy mouth; but thou shalt meditate therein day and night, that thou mayest observe to do according to all that is written therein: for then thou shalt make thy way prosperous, and then thou shalt have good success.

⁹ Have not I commanded thee? Be strong and of a good courage; be not afraid, neither be thou dismayed: for the Lord thy God is with thee whithersoever thou goest.

Deuteronomy 31:8
And the Lord, he it is that doth go before thee; he will be with thee, he will not fail thee, neither forsake thee: fear not, neither be dismayed.

1 Chronicles 28:20
And David said to Solomon his son, Be strong and of good courage, and do it: fear not, nor be dismayed: for the Lord God, even my God, will be with thee; he will not fail thee, nor forsake thee, until thou hast finished all the work for the service of the house of the Lord.

Yes that is correct: Do not be afraid to fail. In life, there will be some failures, and that's the real truth!

Failure is part of human reality. So often, we live in a semi-fantasy world of denial of what is actually taking place in our lives and all around us, while a *reality check* says that we must look at and deal with the facts of life as they truly are.

We can get a better appreciation for how important it is to accept the occasional failure, because in life there will be some disappointing outcomes – that is the reality of it. So it makes no sense to stick our proverbial heads in the sand, hoping it will go away, while the rest of our body is exposed to the stark truth.

Now, what we have to do is learn how to deal with it, and the Lord knew that the fear of failure is one of the most crippling things that come against the great purposes in our lives. That is why He dealt with it very early in the commissioning of Joshua for the task he was called to do. As a matter of fact, the theme of the first 9 verses of Joshua chapter 1 (above) is encouragement and exhortation against the fear of failure. Well! If the Lord knows that the only thing that can keep us from accomplishment is the fear of failure, should we not step over this fear and begin to accomplish what we have been commissioned on the earth to do?

You see the fear of failure looks at all of the possible negative results and totally ignores the positive outcomes, and even moreso ignores the greatness that lies within each one of us and that propels us to success and victory!

I say to my readers, for this is specifically prepared for you without any fear of failure or of contradiction, *stop being afraid to fail, Stop Being Afraid to Fail, STOP BEING AFRAID TO FAIL* – in the name of JESUS!

This fear has kept you down and kept you locked up for too long, and thus saith the Lord. It is time for the readers of this word to rise up and stop being afraid to fail. The fear of failure brings a lot of excuses and blame casting, but today you will rise to a new level of thinking and a new attitude, and that is one of a positive "I can do it with the Lord at my side" mindset. Remember the words of the Lord to Joshua. Read our scripture again, and see how the Lord speaks of success and failure.

Too many lives lost, too many dreams dashed. Too many great people sitting on the roadside of life without hope because of this thing. Too many people drunk or high or sick just because of this fear. Let the Lord Jesus Christ take you to a new place today, let the Lord take you out of fear and into his marvelous light.

I declare that I am bold, accomplished, valuable and victorious!

I take my perspective from the Lord whose thoughts towards me are good and not evil, to give me an expected (good) end.

Strength in Failure

Romans 8:28
And we know that all things work together for good to them that love God, to them who are the called according to His purpose.

Proverbs 24:16
For a just man falleth seven times, and riseth up again: but the wicked shall fall into mischief.

We have looked at 'not being afraid to fail' and here we will look at the subject from a different perspective: 'Strength in Failure'. Now, this might seem a bit controversial to those who are quick to criticize, but those of us who live the realities of life have come to realize that, even in failure, the Lord is able to draw out some degree of strength from us that we did not even know we possessed before.

I am not advocating failure as a lifestyle, far from it! But I am pointing to the fact that the Lord is able to and often does turn what we call *failures* into great successes in ways we never imagined possible.

Have you ever made a wrong turn and thought that you missed your destination – only to find a surprise treasure that *only* making that wrong turn could reveal?

Have you ever made a mistake and everyone including you thought that it was the end of the world – but it turned out amazingly well when combined with other new events coming on its heels? This could very well be your version of 'a silver lining in every dark cloud'!

The promise to those who love God in steadfast certainty is a word of encouragement to those who think that all is lost. It says in our scripture,

"And we know that all things work together for good to them that love God, to them whose are the called according to His purpose."

One quick thing we learn from this scripture is that our failures do not derail or deny the fulfillment of God's purpose in our life, and that alone is cause to rejoice, for our God is so powerful and awesome that even failures are useful.

Now that is very good, but the part that I like for personal development, maturity and growth in spiritual and temporal life is this scripture, for it applies in all avenues.

Proverbs 24:16 (above) tells us of the strength of a 'just man' to rise again and again.

You must be that just man, which means to have a right relationship with the Lord as your Saviour. Next, it is inevitable that several falls will come along in life. Next your rise from each fall – and here is where the key to strength is – shows a certain amount of fortitude and determination to rise up after each fall and to keep going. For if you are not going anywhere or doing anything, you will not have any place to fall from; likewise, without a direction and purpose, why get up again?

The strength that you muster comes from the grace of God; you rise and keep going in spite of the critics and the distractions of the fall. That you are headed someplace with a determination of getting there means that the fall is never as distracting to you as the need to rise again is compelling!

Do you see now the strength and benefits of failure or falling? It reveals in us a deeper level of character than we ever knew before. I also submit to you that those who have fallen and risen again are *least likely* to fall again any time soon. This can also teach others how not to give up when they fall, for falling is not always a bad thing, while staying down is always a detrimental choice.

Today if you hear the voice of the Lord calling you from where you have fallen, please obey his voice and get up! Return to the Lord, for He will abundantly pardon. Do not allow the failures in your life to keep you from the next victory, allow the Lord to help you to gain strength from your weaknesses. So you tried and failed, so what now? Go ahead and try again, that's what! This time might just be your time of success.

> *I **declare** that the spirit of perseverance will outlast any occurrence of failure and defeat in my life.*

> *I **will pursue** my goals with a passion which will not faint in face of any obstacle.*

> *I **know** that the Lord cares for me, therefore I **will allow** that truth to sustain me each time I need strength to get up again.*

Support, Abandonment, Belief

The human creatures that we are often get overtaken by our too-abundant supply of negative, heavy feelings. It is at times like these that we feel we cannot go on.

Sometimes a great grief or loss has befallen us, or a great failure has been ours to bear, or an illness has hit us hard and stolen all our energy. And we fall into this 'fog' of feeling sorry for ourselves and totally abandoned by His Son. No one is able to talk sense into us or shake us out of this morass.

We are also unable to pray or read the Word. Because we cannot take up our Bible or even get peaceful enough to pray, it seems as though these burdensome feelings keep us from our connection with the Lord. The feelings would have us believe that we have been abandoned by Him. Feelings of depression or heaviness are like thick brick walls between us and our beliefs in the Lord, His wisdom and His omnipresence with us.

Take courage! Take heart! Although *you* may not be able to hear His Voice at this moment in time, *He* is listening to you all the time. Just say something simple to Him, such as, "I am letting you pull me closer to you, dear Lord". And then let it be so.

Is He Deaf?

Isaiah 59:1
[1] *Behold, the Lord's hand is not shortened, that it cannot save; neither his ear heavy, that it cannot hear*
[2] *But your iniquities have separated between you and your God, and your sins have hid his face from you, that he will not hear.*

Unbelief is easy to creep into our minds. We are so used to depending on what we see with our eyes or touch with our hands that it becomes too much for us to depend on a simple belief, and moreso a simple belief in God. The time is now, when only a personal relationship with the Lord Jesus Christ will be able to bring the peace and assurance that will take us through life. Anything else is simply lacking all of the necessary ingredients.

Sure, other options might have numerous answers and helps, but the only complete solution is in the Lord Jesus Christ. This brings us to our scripture from Isaiah in the first verse – is the Lord's hand really shortened? Is it unable to save? Is His ear really heavy such that it cannot hear?

The answer is found in the second verse: *Your iniquities have separated between you and your God, and your sins have hid His face from you, that He will not hear.* The reason we turn from the Jesus option is because of our sins and iniquities. That is because we know in our hearts that sin is what separates us from God and we cover it up by saying His hand is short and His ear is heavy.

Often times it is secret sins of our thought life. Many people sin in their thoughts and the sin is never revealed on the outside, but secret sin as well as open sin separates you from God! There is no hiding from Him, even if you keep the thing buried in your heart and ordinary mind.

So we come to the place where it is hard to believe God because we fool ourselves with the thought that "I am okay, so it must be God that is deaf." This also is unbelief, for we are refusing to believe that repentance is needed for our secret sins. Oh sure, the outward show might look glorious, but the poison in the heart keeps the real joy away; it keeps the connection with God away. It eats away at you on the inside and you still harden your heart and blame God for being deaf. What a state of unbelief!

The victorious heart is the one that will say, "I need to make a change, I need to be honest with myself and with God, I need the help that only comes from Jesus." With this type of attitude, the Lord will help – He will heal, He will forgive, because He is willing to listen and able to save those that will come to Him in true belief of Him as Saviour.

Again, the message is *"only believe"* – believe that you need Him, believe that He can hear and save you. Believe that He is ever-present.

> **Lord help** my unbelief! **I declare** that I will allow the center of my belief to recognize that God is a Spirit and I must worship Him in spirit and in truth. This realization will bring me into the connection needed for my growth and blessings found in Him.

Only Believe

John 11:40

Jesus saith unto her, Said I not unto thee, that, if thou wouldest believe, thou shouldest see the glory of God?

We all have personal struggles in life, and most of the time the greatest struggle we face is the one to simply *believe*.

This is often the case because we humans need so much "real" proof to reach beyond the doubts to that point of simply believing. To simply believe in its purest form is to just let go, to just let go of all the doubts, cares, fears and worries and simply believe.

Remember when Peter wanted to walk on the water and Jesus told him to come, he had to simply believe that he could walk on water and he did, until the cares and fears were allowed to step back in and he began to sink. My dear readers, he had the power over the cares and fears and exercised his belief in the word given by Jesus and that is why he could walk on the water in the first place.

We today face the same controversy when it comes to simply believing Jesus. We struggle to "let go and let God"; we try too hard to analyze instead of simply trusting God in pure belief. We are too afraid to walk by Faith. We need the reassurance of sight, but sight cannot go where Faith goes and cannot accomplish what Faith accomplishes, for Faith does work in the spiritual while sight is limited to the natural realm only. That is why the Word of God tells us to walk by Faith and not by sight.

In our text from John, Jesus is emphasizing the fact that it is our belief that will move the mighty hand of God – not our sight, not our ability, but simply our belief. Now this is both a simple and complex concept all at one time. Complex, because of all the things in our psychological and emotional make-up that we have to let go of. Simple, because it works as soon as we get it right, as soon as we finally learn to truly let go. There are no further hoops to jump through. There are no additional requirements. It just works as Jesus said. We will see the Glory of God on our behalf and in every situation, if we can only reach that place to just believe.

> *I declare* that I will allow the transforming power of God to usher me into new realms of living as I renew my mind to walk by faith and not by sight.

> *I accept* the truth that all things are possible to someone who believes.

Press...for a Breakthrough

I Samuel 30:6
And David was greatly distressed; for the people spake of stoning him, because the soul of all the people was grieved, every man for his sons and for his daughters: but David encouraged himself in the Lord his God.

1 Chronicles 29:17
I know also, my God, that thou triest the heart, and hast pleasure in uprightness. As for me, in the uprightness of mine heart I have willingly offered all these things: and now have I seen with joy thy people, which are present here, to offer willingly unto thee.

Nehemiah 8:10
[...] for the joy of the LORD is your strength.

This message today is for all those who feel tired in body, soul and spirit and who contemplate giving up. You are tempted to give up on yourself, on your children, on your entire family perhaps. To give up on your faith, your church congregation and on your churchgoing. To give up on the Lord. I speak to those who are thinking, "I just can't do it anymore, this just is not working..."

For those who have tried and tried and tried again and it seems like God is deaf – if you fit any of these categories or a similar one, be encouraged! Take courage! You are closer than you think. Do not allow the spirit of tiredness, rejection and dejection get hold of you any longer, but cast it off with joy, yes joy!

You see, joy is the antidote or medicine which fixes the tired, give-it-all-up mentality. Joy is light, explosive and energizing, and it disintegrates that spirit of heaviness that makes us want to stop the car and get off of the road of life.

I am here to tell you this morning that what you are going through is not strange. It isn't even unusual, but is similar to what all others go through at some point. Joy is the solution.

"How can I get joy", you ask. Well our texts tell us the most important step: we must have a mindset for joy; we must have a determination for joy, even as weak as we feel, and encourage ourselves in the Lord. *This is both a committed decision and an internal struggle!* We do not look for someone else to become our crutch or support. We must become self-encouragers and allow the joy of that attitude to explode around us and destroy the spirit of heaviness that wants to steal our destiny.

One of the main reasons we get hit with a spirit of heaviness is because our breakthrough is very, very close. Sometimes it is the enemy, sometimes it is simply our own battle fatigue kicking in. Whatever the reason, giving up is a losing proposition, so do not give up!

The Bible has many encouraging words such as 'weeping may endure for a night, but joy cometh in the morning'. 'The joy of the Lord is my strength, the garment of praise removes the spirit of heaviness'. 'Shout, for the Lord has given you the city!' Again, this is not a time to give up or throw in the towel.

Instead, press, press, press for your breakthrough. It must have been valuable for you to have started in the first place, and have you now come this far only to dare to give up?

I say to you NO WAY, you will not give up! But instead you will gain the victory through Jesus Christ the Lord. So press, press, press, until you get your joy back and march through in the strength of that joy to the victory that is close at hand, I say to you PRESS ON!

I declare *to myself I'm a winner not a loser, a victor not a victim, I'm encouraged not discouraged!*

I know *that I have the God-given ability to turn my bad into good, my good into better and my better into best.*

I take control *of that which controls me and shout hallelujah! I've got joy!*

Material Things

We live in consumer societies. This means that there is a wealth of material possessions beckoning to us, tempting us, which we can usually purchase at relatively small cost in relation to our earnings. If not, we are more than happy to go into debt just to have the thing! We can collect lots of clothing, lots of electronic devices, lots of "stuff". We can subscribe to any number of services for our person, our homes, our workplaces. All we do is pay!

But the Christian must ask himself if material possessions – and especially the pursuit of them – have taken over his life. I am not by any means saying, as the Christ did in one example of true riches, to give it all away. But as Christians, we have an opportunity to bring things into balance and perspective in Christ. Just as the Rich Young Ruler resisted the Lord's directive to "give it all up", so does modern man have such resistance to either giving it all up or not purchasing it in the first place.

What is the Lord's guidance for you personally regarding accumulation of worldly goods? As with Christ's truth, which comes from great simplicity, secure eternal (spiritual) riches first and foremost. The Lord's guidance may lead you back to great material simplicity, but not as objects of worship. Read scripture. Pray. Listen and act upon His simple truth, and upon His guidance.

Real Blessing

Psalms 32:1

[1] *Blessed is he whose transgression is forgiven, whose sin is covered.*

[2] *Blessed is the man unto whom the Lord imputeth not iniquity, and in whose spirit there is no guile.*

We live in a day and time in which blessings are being defined as the giving and receiving of material things and money. People are now measuring the favour and blessing of God by how many things and how much money they possess. So if you are not endowed with what the world thinks is a good amount of such things, you are considered not to be blessed.

A blessing is anything that comes as God's favor. It can come in the form of another individual's support. It can be something you ask God for and receive. It can be something that you have in your life – a possession, a person or a circumstance – for which you are grateful, and recognize as being bestowed upon you by God. The issue of our blessings is so messed up today that we forget to count the blessing of protection and health given by the Lord. We go about everyday assuming that it is all created by us on our own strength and goodness, and we totally forget the Lord Jesus Christ who is there providing our daily protection, health and strength. God's protection is also, then, considered a blessing, as in a healthy body or a safe home – or a transgression that is forgiven.

The spiritual blessing is thus far more than simply possession of things. The Bible blessing is on the personal level, the empowerment by God to each person to get possessions and wealth by accepted and lawful means. Any other way is not a blessing, for it will surely become a snare and curse to you in the long run.

The Bible blessing is so valuable, for what can be more valuable than to have your sins and transgressions forgiven? What can be more valuable than to experience the peace of God that passes all understanding? Do we really appreciate peace? Do we know what is real peace? For so long people have lived in turmoil, fear, torment, worries and the like that to them peace has become a day when the level of such things is not quite so high. But real peace that passes all understanding radiates from the inside and is the blessing from God.

> *I declare* the Peace of God over my life, family, workplace and community, that peace which the Lord giveth, not as the world giveth. Therefore, I will not let my heart be troubled or be afraid. I take this day to move forward with the reassurance of good success in all endeavors, for that is a real blessing!

Pleasing the Crowd

Mark 15:15

And so Pilate, willing to content the people, released Barabbas unto them, and delivered Jesus, when he had scourged him, to be crucified.

Isn't it strange the motives behind certain actions? How many times have we purchased a possession only to impress one or more other people? How many times have we agreed to participate in an event or do something for a group only in order to get that pat on the back?

We have here a situation which is played out daily to some degree or another in our lives. An action being taken, not because it is the right action, not because it is your decision, not because it is what your heart tells you to do, but just to *please the crowd*.

Now if your life depended on it, you might say well it is understandable, but when you are in a position to receive no hurt for doing what is morally correct. Regardless of what the crowd might think and say, you are obligated to do the right thing.

Pilate in this instance had the power of choice, but he gave that up when he gave in to the demands of the people and not the demands of his heart. He not only condemned Jesus to death, but he condemned his own self – for if your heart condemns you, then you are guilty indeed!

The real problem here is not that of Jesus going to the cross – that is, as we know, the reason for which He came, to give His life as a ransom for many. No, no. The problem is that Pilate allowed popular opinion to cloud his judgment when it became time to choose.

An even sadder truth is that people today, just like Pilate back then, still allow popular opinion to cloud their judgment in making decisions concerning Jesus Christ. That is the crux of the matter as you read this! You see we live in a world where popularity and public opinion has become more valuable than standing for what will really last.

People would rather dwell in the tents for wickedness that to be a doorkeeper in the House of the Lord. We find if we are truly honest, most people reject giving their lives to Jesus because of the perception the crowd has of such a lifestyle...

> *I declare that I will not be ashamed of the gospel of Christ, for indeed it is the power of God's salvation unto everyone that believeth. I also do not want the Lord to be ashamed to own me when He cometh in glory with the holy angels.*

> *I will, in a decent manner, let friends, family and community know the Jesus is the Way, the Truth, the Life, and the only way to the Father.*

Be Careful How You Obtain What You Have

John 10:1-2

¹ Verily, verily, I say unto you, He that entereth not by the door into the sheepfold, but climbeth up some other way, the same is a thief and a robber.
² But he that entereth in by the door is the shepherd of the sheep.

In this world of instant gratification, with mankind driven as it were to have all things accomplished in as short a time as possible, we oftentimes tend to miss the deeper issues and core values of the experiences we have, purely because we rush through everything.

Now, the present atmosphere on the earth is to rush-rush, hurry-hurry – but in so doing we find that so many mistakes are made that could have otherwise been avoided. This is because we don't take the time to sit down and consider, the time to wait and see if anything else must be taken into account, the time to pray, wait, and hear from God. Extra time "to get it right" is just not a contributing element of decision-making or action-taking in the rush-rush atmosphere in the earth today.

It seems that especially prayer and waiting on God is a no-no these days; it is almost as if you become an enemy of society if you say "I am going to pray and wait on the Lord before I make this decision." Though you want to do it, you are pressured.

But I believe, that there are still some people left on earth who are not afraid to claim the Lord Jesus Christ in all areas of their lives, regardless of what others may have to say.

This rush-rush atmosphere has led persons into decisions and situations which cause blame and shame, brokenness and poverty, broken homes and severed relationships, headache and heartbreak – simply because the time to think and pray it through did not measure up to the glitter, adrenaline rush and instant gratification presented.

This said, we must be careful of how we come by the things we possess, and more importantly of how we come by our relationship with God.

Our text warns us that if we try to enter God's kingdom any other way but the right way we are thieves and robbers. This is serious business when it comes to our soul salvation! The trend of the world is that we can just say a few quick words and that will take care of the God requirement. Remember though, the system of seeking the Lord with fear and trembling in prayer still works; it has been proven, and it brings real results.

There are some things that lend themselves to the quick fix, but salvation is not one of those things. Do not be fooled, dear readers: to find the Lord we must first *seek* Him. This is not a microwave business! A repentant heart, a willing heart, a contrite heart and spirit will find the Lord. Do not put off the Lord for some more convenient time. Take the time out of your busy schedule and seek the Lord until you find Him. It is worth it for Time and Eternity.

> *I declare* that I will no longer harden my heart to the voice of the Lord. As His Spirit speaks to me, I will yield and obey and no longer act as those did in the provocation when tempted in the wilderness.
>
> *I know* that with Christ all things are possible if I only believe.

Put God First

It has been my observation that when things go awry with any individual, family or community, there is one source for that trouble. It is this: Instead of putting God first, they have put something else in first place. In other words, they don't have their priorities straight.

It has also been my observation that when an individual, family or community puts God first, things mostly go right, and the best outcomes unfold in great harmony and happiness.

Many Christians with their priorities in the right place might say, "God first, then family, then work. And if there is time, then other people and all the rest." Let me be clear that God first within the family is the motive, as we commune with God for and with family.

Too many of us need to return to putting God first – and it is very simple to do so. Start your day in quiet communion with the Lord. Read a Scripture, and ask the Lord to make it clear to you how that Scripture applies to your life here and now and today. Remember your worries and troubles, and surrender them to Christ the Lord... if only for that day. And then? Do it again tomorrow!

By putting God first, He makes everything right with your day. He creates time for everything on your agenda. He creates time for you to be with everyone that you love. He smooths your path, reducing or eliminating the number of problems that you might encounter. By putting God first, all comes right in your world.

Every Mountain and Hill Shall Be Brought Low...

Luke 3:5-6
5 Every valley shall be filled, and every mountain and hill shall be brought low; and the crooked shall be made straight, and the rough ways shall be made smooth;
6 And all flesh shall see the salvation of God.

Part of the beauty of the Virgin Islands is in her hills, not just the hills by themselves, but the way God has made them to cascade to the sea shore creates a wonderful picture – so much so that people pay to enjoy the scenery.

Now, the fact is that hills are hard to climb, difficult to cultivate, you must dig rows and bank the dirt with stone and rock walls. Hills are difficult to build a house on, you must first dig into the side of the hill to get a ledge to place your foundation and so on. To put it bluntly, hills look nice but they are not so nice for practical living. They are in fact hard to deal with and it costs a lot of time, energy, money and patience to work with a hill.

Now, we come to the hills in life. We all know of the difficulties that we encounter from time to time, which we also may call trials, challenges, problems, tests, issues or tribulations ... I suppose these are good descriptions, because a challenge means that you must rise to meet it (climb that hill) and overcome it (reach the summit).

The thing that I like about the Holy Scriptures is that all of the answers to life – spanning all of the ages, responding to all the types of issues we could possibly face, and affecting all men and women – are found in them. Now the Bible says that *'Every mountain and hill shall be brought low...'* Armed with this assurance, we can apply that mentality to our personal hills and move forward with the attitude that every hill presented to us can be climbed and conquered.

Believing that every challenge shall be brought low – that is, brought within our ability to conquer it – takes steadfast faith. The Bible tells us that Faith comes by hearing the Word of God. The Word points right back to itself even as it points us forward in faith, hope and love for God. In God, we are guided to the best way for us at this moment in time for meeting and overcoming our hills. Only the Lord can do that – point us in many directions and still propel us forward and *through* our problem, with a solution discovered by Faith.

The point of learning and growth is *not* the hill or challenge! The point is in the approach you take (turning to the Word and the Lord's guiding hand) and the solution you implement through your faith (doing as guided even when you cannot see how it could possibly work out). The solution found in putting God and His solution first. Faith when facing all of life's hills will bring them low and manageable.

> *I declare to possess a faith which will say to my hills and mountains 'be thou removed and be cast into the sea...'*
> *In life, there will be tribulations, but I agree with Jesus to be of good cheer because He has overcome the world, in Him I too will overcome.*

The Desire to Seek After God

> **Psalm 42: 1-3**
> *1 As the hart panteth after the water brooks, so panteth my soul after thee, O God.*
> *2 My soul thirsteth for God, for the living God: when shall I come and appear before God?*
> *3 My tears have been my meat day and night, while they continually say unto me, Where is thy God?*

In the **42nd Psalm**, we have the heartfelt words of a man whose passion and every *desire* was not only to seek after God but to truly get into His Presence. These are not idle words, but they express as much as possible by way of the written word, what we cannot so often express in words, and that is the conditions of our emotions that drive us and which is so hard to get others to understand.

David tried to give his best explanation of this desire for God and we are left with not only a lasting impression but we are also left with a spiritual yearning he had to fulfill his desire. Reach for your Bible and read the entire **42nd Psalm**.

This is not a passing fancy. We are told to put God first and to keep Him first! We cannot sustain that effort without a burning desire. We must have a desire for God which will be the fuel or energy source to keep Him first. Without this desire, our best intentions, our best efforts, all of our well-meaning attempts to keep God first will soon die out and become a thing of the past. But desire will keep the fire burning.

Do you remember when you had that desire to see the one you love, and nothing seemed too much in order to satisfy that desire? No distance was too long, no hour was too late, no gift was too expensive to satisfy that desire that could only be quenched by the presence of your object of love. So also, we must desire after God and not be satisfied until we enter into His presence.

God will feel this desire and will turn and also pursue us. It is a lovely thing, He turns His attention to you; that is what it takes. We wish for God, but we do not have that passionate desire. When He shows up, everything becomes all right. Whenever God steps in, He makes all wrongs to become right.

Our *constant desire* is important, because so often we only want God to show up when it is convenient for us, when we have a situation that we know only He could solve. But if we keep Him first, we will not need to be so desperate. We will have the peace and assurance that He is with us.

Let Desire be your watchword. Let that passionate desire push you into His presence daily!

> *I declare* *that my overwhelming desire will always be to dwell (spiritually) in the presence of the Lord. In His presence, my joy becomes full and pleasures abound. The circumstances that stress my human abilities are swallowed up by the awesome peace which radiates from His presence.*

First Things First
A 4-Part Presentation for Young Adults

Romans 12:2
And be not conformed to this world: but be ye transformed by the renewing of your mind, that ye may prove what is that good, and acceptable, and perfect, will of God.

Romans 6:12-13
[12] Let not sin therefore reign in your mortal body, that ye should obey it in the lusts thereof.
[13] Neither yield ye your members as instruments of un-righteousness unto sin: but yield yourselves unto God, as those that are alive from the dead, and your members as instruments of righteousness unto God.

Romans 6:16
Know ye not, that to whom ye yield yourselves servants to obey, his servants ye are to whom ye obey; whether of sin unto death, or of obedience unto righteousness?

Truly Putting God First
"Renewing" sometimes means that you have got to change your mindset and some of your beliefs, that your state of mind is incorrect in Christ. It takes an act of will to make a change, and this is possible because God gave us complete control of our own will. In this world, we easily see that there are consequences to yielding to the wrong master. Drug addiction, sexual perversions, stealing others' property or attacking other individuals, lying, and all repeated willful sin – all these represent caving into the wrong master. There are consequences to turning away from the righteousness of the Lord.

By renewing your mind, you more easily also change the way you react to all things. You come from understanding, love and Christ-like compassion. This will not make you weak! Quite the contrary, it gives you untold inner strength. While it is easier to complain than to praise or easier to lash out at someone than to keep silent, that compassion will allow you to bite your tongue and reflect before taking any action.

> *I declare* *that I can make my way in life clean and purposeful by taking heed to the Word of God. At this age, it is important to avoid unnecessary mistakes and the best guide for minimizing mistakes is the Word of God.* *I am thankful* *for this instruction.*

> *I declare* *a full and victorious end because of my obedience.*

Being a Good Steward

A steward is simply a manager. A caretaker. We are, each of us, the steward of our God-given talents and abilities. We are, each of us, the steward of the wealth (or lack thereof) that we are able to create in this world, and the steward of our material possessions.

God has put into each of us a gift to use, helping us to carry out the purpose that He has made us for. We are called upon by the Lord to give an account of the stewardship of that gift.

As we put "first things first", we must seek out God in our prayers as He tells or shows us our purpose. As we move into that personal purpose, our gifts will develop and grow to meet its demands.

Putting God first means letting God guide you in the fulfillment of His purpose for your life. Putting first things first, you follow the Lord's guidance and thus avoid the source of most of life's frustrations, illnesses, and miseries – as they come from living outside of or separate from your God-given purpose.

> *I declare* that I will stand on my watch and faithfully execute the instructions of the Lord concerning my stewardship.
>
> *I know* that I must give an account, and I want to hear 'well done good and faithful servant'. *I appreciate* the trust placed in me by the Lord, to whom all things truly belong.

Importance of Speaking the Word

The written Word (logos) can be read and memorized, but not until it is spoken (rhema) does it have life in application. Certain things without life is useless, but life creates activity, and activity brings results. The Word of God has the quality that makes it come to life. Speaking the Word in confession, prayer, song, and declaration/commands is how you wield the Sword of the Spirit. This is our offensive/attack weapon

It is effective because the Word says God watches over the (spoken) Word to perform it, to guarantee that it will not return void or ineffective, but will accomplish what it was sent (spoken) to do.

The Word of God also says that the angels hearken to the voice of the spoken Word to take action.

> *I declare* that I will speak the Word with the faith and knowledge that the Word is spirit and life. That life is a God-inspired quality that allows it to work out the will of God for any situation it is sent into.

> *I gladly put my trust* in the Word and the Lord, which will never fail.

Believe the Word, Learn to Walk by Faith

This again is a decision governed by your own will. Walking by Faith does not mean to do nothing! It means that as you take action, you believe God will make a way even though you see no way when you begin.

To walk by Faith is critical to survival in the current and future state of this earth. To walk by Faith is the only way to truly please God, by showing our dependence on Him to work out the impossible things in life.

> *I declare* that the mystery of Faith being the substance of things hoped for and the evidence of things not seen, is

for me to believe and act upon rather than to explain how it is possible.

My duty *is to believe God without any doubt, and He will bring the results.*

Peace and Goodwill toward Men

When we observe the events occurring in our world – the warfare and violence, the crime and murders, the mayhem and discord – it seems right to wonder whatever happened to our year-end greeting to each other, "Merry Christmas, with *peace* and *goodwill* toward all men!"

Taking actions of goodwill toward our fellow man in need is a conscious decision. It comes from the mind and the heart that you have united in Christ.

Creating peace all around us may seem more complicated, or even impossible! However, when we are willing to adapt a Christ-like mind and way of thinking, we come more often to solutions and resolutions than to conflict and disagreement. We just follow the path set out for us by Jesus.

Creating goodwill and peace is a conscious choice of how to think and how to act. Be led by the example of our Lord Jesus Christ, who makes all things possible – even in seemingly complex and difficult circumstances.

How to Lend unto the Lord

Proverbs 19:17
He that hath pity upon the poor lendeth unto the Lord; and that which he hath given will he pay him again.

Matthew 25:34-40
[34] Then shall the King say unto them on his right hand, Come, ye blessed of my Father, inherit the kingdom prepared for you from the foundation of the world:
[35] For I was hungered, and ye gave me meat: I was thirsty, and ye gave me drink: I was a stranger, and ye took me in:
[36] Naked, and ye clothed me: I was sick, and ye visited me: I was in prison, and ye came unto me.
[37] Then shall the righteous answer him, saying, Lord, when saw we thee hungered, and fed thee? or thirsty, and gave thee drink?
[38] When saw we thee a stranger, and took thee in? or naked, and clothed thee?
[39] Or when saw we thee sick, or in prison, and came unto thee?
[40] And the King shall answer and say unto them, Verily I say unto you, Inasmuch as ye have done it unto one of the least of these my brethren, ye have done it unto me.

Sometimes we do things without the full understanding of what we are actually doing. We go about performing acts of kindness and goodwill to those in need, and oftentimes think that it is just us, taking specific actions.

But the Lord has a way of using the goodness of our hearts to bless us, even without our realizing it. Now, our scripture points out a very powerful concept, a concept that is more secure than the stock market or the banks. It points out that we can actually *lend unto the Lord.* Yes, we all know that the Lord is not in need of anything. But actually, He needs for us to *have a Heart like His*. That is His great desire, that we become more like Him.

How does this all work to our benefit? Well, first of all, our heart has to be in the right place. We cannot give to the needy just to exact a Blessing from the Lord! We cannot think, "I gave, so now the scripture says that I have lent unto the Lord and that He will pay me."

But a heart of true compassion, with pure motives, will touch the heart of God and the benefit will be ours. You ask, "How do I have assurance that the Lord receives that act of kindness as unto Him." Read again our scripture from **Matthew.** Yes, it is true we give as unto the Lord of our time, talent, and money, and He receives it as unto Himself when we use the heart of Christ and do it unto *"the least of these my brethren"*.

We cannot see the Lord, but we do see our fellow man every day. Will we now use the method given to us to give to the Lord by taking care of the needs of our fellow man? Think about it.

> *I decide to touch the heart of God by making my heart empty of selfish desires and act in the interest of the Will of God. The benefits of a pure heart will be mine because God considers the heart not the outward appearance.*

Goodwill

Luke 2:13-14

[13] *And suddenly there was with the angel a multitude of the heavenly host praising God, and saying,*
[14] *Glory to God in the highest, and on earth peace, good will toward men.*

The aspect of God that I like the most is how suddenly He moves. The scripture tells us that 'suddenly' there were with the angel a multitude of the heavenly host praising God. Not only was it sudden, it was on a large scale (the multitude) and that is another aspect of how God moves – suddenly, and on a large scale. Think of the magnitude!

There can be no doubt when God is the one who does something, because whatever He does is simply set apart from the ordinary. Indeed, it must be because He is God and besides Him, there is no other.

The peace and goodwill that was extended to us on earth was not for that time only but is present with us continuously. Goodwill is that intangible aspect of life that we benefit from without a physical manifestation. The grace of God is the most apparent aspect of the goodwill brought to earth by Jesus Christ. The grace which enables us to endure trials and injustice, and still smile and say thank you Lord, is just a glimpse of the goodwill benefit toward men.

I believe that if grace and goodwill were tangible, we would fight and kill each other for it – just as we do for gold, diamonds and cash or even land or anything of perceived value.

This is where mankind has messed up the gifts of God by trying always to control them and make them our instruments of power. God, being as only He can be, made goodwill, grace and peace intangible so that we must accept and experience them by faith! Otherwise, we would be doomed to mess that up as we have everything else and we would end up being eternally lost.

O mankind, when will we get it?

> Lord, **give me the ability** to accept your Grace and Goodwill without any ulterior motives. **I understand** that corruption in my heart will block the blessings so freely available to the 'whosoever'.

> Lord, **help me** to remove darkness from my heart and clouds from my mind that I may taste and see that you are good.

What Is Your Calling?

Acts 16:9-10
⁹ And a vision appeared to Paul in the night; There stood a man of Macedonia, and prayed him, saying, Come over into Macedonia, and help us.
¹⁰ And after he had seen the vision, immediately we endeavoured to go into Macedonia, assuredly gathering that the Lord had called us for to preach the gospel unto them.

We all have a certain level of dissatisfaction in life and often times that inner uneasiness or restlessness is the deep part of our spirit calling out to find its' correct place or calling.

Now you may have a very good paying job, a top position where you command respect and authority over all around you. By the standards of the world, you *should* (keyword *should*) be doing well, be prosperous and happy.

But deep inside of you something is calling out, and it shows itself as a sense of uneasiness and dissatisfaction that no one else can know about. No one but you knows you are experiencing it. Now, this is not for everybody, for some of us are so casual and easily relaxing in our current state of false success (yes, *false* success) that we ignore the deeper things of our spirit. Our spirit hears the call and is crying out to answer it.

In our text, Paul was already out doing missions for the Lord, but he had a sensitivity to the spirit that immediately allowed him to change his course and respond to the call.

My question to you today is, 'What is your calling?' What has been nudging your spirit to the point where you are dissatisfied with your present lot in life, even though that is what the world says is success? Do you feel more natural doing something other than what you are doing? Is this something that can still prosper you? Is this something that can be used for the Glory of God? What is your calling? Why have you been so complacent?

Not everyone has the same calling. We need different callings to fill the earth with passion and talent in all spheres of activity. Not everyone can be a preacher, governor or some sort of chief, but you can fulfill your destiny in life if you follow the true calling of your heart. You will be happy and peaceful doing it; it will prosper you.

This inner peace is key to prolonging your life. Do not go to the grave without at least *trying* to fulfill your true destiny and calling! This might call for a radical change in your current direction. To have his own measure of inner peace, Paul also had to change his direction to answer the Macedonian call; the key to his success was that he was in Christ and doing the will of God.

Let your true calling be something that is not sinful, but is of the Lord and something that is your natural ability. The best place to find that calling is from the One who gave it to you in the first place, and that is in the Lord Jesus Christ. The Word of God makes it clear that the only way to God is through the Lord Jesus Christ. Come His way and allow Him to lead you into life everlasting and a life of fulfilling your calling here on earth.

> *I declare* that I will fulfill my calling because God birthed it in me and He is able to complete what He started.

> *I submit* my desires to my God-given calling, knowing that true peace comes from being in unison with the plan of God for me and by extension those who benefit.

Waking Up, Seeing and New Awareness

So many of us are wandering around like automatons!

We look out into our world, but don't see the greater truths embedded in its events – we don't connect the dots between seemingly complex world "problems" and the highest sort of spiritually-based solutions to them.

We interact on a superficial and surface level only with other humans – texting, tweeting and instant messaging – remaining within social conventions and political correctness. That just means we have no true spiritual connection with people or significant conversation with them.

How can this be? It is so, because we have not awakened to the Lord Jesus Christ, His guidance, His word – and thus we cannot obey it. As we are not awakened to Him, we are not "tuned in to His radio station" and do not hear when He speaks. We do not see the path that He has opened before us because we are not "viewing His movie."

Our spiritual eyes are closed. Our spiritual heart is sleeping. Our human mind only presents that to us which makes rational sense to it – and "faith" has no place in the ordinary human mind which demands proofs of all kinds, right?

Wake up to Christ! Wake up to the call of your spirit, through whom the Lord speaks and guides you. There is more to this world of ours and the people in it than meets your physical eyes and senses.

Jacob's Well – the Well of Sychar

> **John 4:4-6**
> *⁴ And he must needs go through Samaria.*
> *⁵ Then cometh he to a city of Samaria, which is called Sychar, near to the parcel of ground that Jacob gave to his son Joseph.*
> *⁶ Now Jacob's Well was there. Jesus therefore, being wearied with his journey, sat thus on the well: and it was about the sixth hour.*

The first thing we notice about this scripture is that there is a connotation of extra effort – *a detour* – being placed on the route that the Lord takes to get to where He is going. Now it is implied that He could have gotten to Galilee from Judea by a route that did not take him through Samaria, but the Word says He needed to go through Samaria.

Now there are several thoughts that accompany that statement. Samaria is not a place the Jews would naturally frequent, because of the animosity that existed between the Jews and Samaritans. The spiritual needs in that place superseded the natural barriers of human and cultural feelings. The opportune time to meet the woman who would carry the evangelism message of *"Come, see a man…"* was a now time, not a wait-until-later time, because the deliverance was not for her only, but for the entire city. It also gave the opportunity to dispel the false notions of what true worship was for her and her people. So Jesus needed to go through Samaria.

Sometimes in life, we have to go through our own Samaria, and we will question, "Why this route Lord, why can't I achieve this goal some other way, some easier way?" But if we see the big picture that the Lord sees, we will realize that often times our Samaria experience is not for us but for others – perhaps for our entire generation or our entire city or nation, or church or family. Our Samaria experience is by God's divine choosing and timing and all that we have to do to make it successful is to take it patiently and try to learn as much as we can from the experience. God always has more for us than meets the eye! If we are the neutral observer, each of our experiences occurs for multiple (as opposed to just one obvious) reasons!

That is why to follow Him is a walk of faith, trust and confidence – and open-minded analysis. We almost always come to the place where we too can say, "Come see a Man, and Man called Christ Jesus..."

> *I declare* that as I am freed from my bondages of sin, I too will become an evangelist with the clarion call 'come see a man...Christ Jesus!' The Lord has left all to redeem me and *I will do all I can* to declare Him as Lord and Savior.

I Love the Lord

Acts 17:27-28

[27] *That they should seek the Lord, if haply they might feel after him, and find him, though he be not far from every one of us:*

[28] *For in him we live, and move, and have our being; as certain also of your own poets have said, For we are also his offspring.*

Psalm 37:4

Delight thyself also in the Lord: and he shall give thee the desires of thine heart.

Wake up! It's His Love that keeps us, "For in him we live, and move, and have our being;"

The Lord truly is gracious and long-suffering towards us, because the level of unappreciative behavior would have caused the best human to forget us long ago!

For Thanksgiving 2016, my family and I went home to Tortola BVI. After shopping and other errands on the eve of Thanksgiving, we arrived home at 2:00 pm. The power was off at our home. We did chores and 3 hours later power was still off. I checked the meter point to ensure that we weren't disconnected and it was intact. A few minutes later, a Power Utility truck came into the neighborhood but left before I could flag him down.

We prepared for a night of darkness. I prayed silently for power to be restored and called the power company; it was now after working hours.

A friend whom I had not spoken to for many years answered and immediately recognized my voice and addressed me by name (wow!).

We chatted and 10 minutes later power to our neighborhood was restored. I sat down and wrote this devotional account because I want you to know that "I Love the Lord" – moments like these are priceless.

Take the time to allow your faith to supersede your circumstance. True faith does not consider circumstance, just our unshakable belief that the Lord will come through for us. As we gain these type of experiences, our love and warmth found in the richness of our relationship will strengthen and encourage us to keep on living by faith. As we do, our Love for the Lord blossoms into appreciation for the wonderful simplicity of life in Christ. Do you Love Him?

> *I declare that the Lord is able to do exceedingly, abundantly above all than I can ask or think according to the power dwelling in me. This power is resident by my absolute faith and trust in the Lord. Therefore, I declare divine favor and uncommon breakthroughs.*

How Close are We?

Romans 13:11
And that, knowing the time, that now it is high time to awake out of sleep: for now is our salvation nearer than when we believed.

The anxious moments just before a big event always bring what we call butterflies, or some little feeling of nervousness or uneasiness. Events like facing the dentist, the needle from the nurse, the crowd gathered to hear you speak or whatever similar situation, those anxious moments bring us to a place of realization that we are not as strong as we thought we were. We realize that it is possible to make mistakes; we feel some intimidation from the crowd, or the pressure to put on a brave face.

These are the times your strong relationship with Jesus, allows you to simply put all your trust in Him; you know He will see you through. And when the ordeal is over and you see that you are still alive, you breathe a great sigh of relief and say to yourself, "That really wasn't all that bad after all."

I want us to focus in on those anxious moments before we go through what we are facing and relate it to our present condition in Christ. The verse of scripture says *'...for now is our salvation nearer than when we believed'.* This is the time for examining ourselves as in those anxious moments and see that without Jesus we do not have the strength to make it. This is where total dependency on God is needed; this is where our faith should soar high, because we are to see at this point in our lives there is no other source or way to make it outside of Jesus. This is the time when *our salvation is nearer than ever before.*

The alternative offered by the world is not going to work in the long run. We are in the world but not of the world, therefore we have to awaken out of sleep, awaken to the fact that we have to operate in a way that is different to the world. When the world says it is impossible, we have to say, "I will pray about it, for with God all things are possible". When the world says forget about it, we have to say, "I will make my wrongs right", and when the world says this is too much for you, we have to say, "I cast my burdens upon the Lord". When the world says give up there is no hope, we have to say, "Great is thy Faithfulness O God my Father." In short, we must operate from dependency on Jesus, because the time of our salvation is nearer that when we first believed.

Our salvation in this context is not the forgiveness of sin, for the scripture is speaking to believers, but our salvation here is the victory in various struggles and battles in life. Our salvation is the deliverance out of that thing which has so often plagued us. Now is our salvation (our victory, our song of triumph, our joy, our deliverance) nearer than ever before. What a joy to trust in the Lord! No wonder the songwriter said, *'Tis so sweet to trust in Jesus.'*

This in no way excludes the sinner out there! If you do not have a strong relationship allowing you to cast your burdens on the Lord Jesus Christ, as you have often heard, today is the best day to create that relationship! Yes, you hear it all the time, and the reason you keep on hearing it is because it is the truth. No one is trying to force you or control you; we just want you to experience the peace and joy of knowing Jesus as Lord and Saviour.

> *I declare* *that the hour of my deliverance is at hand. My breakthrough is next, my heart is fixed for the change from struggle to victory. My attitude of perseverance will pay off in success! The Lord is on my side, things are getting brighter day by day.*

A Wake Up Call!

I Corinthians 15:34

Awake to righteousness, and sin not; for some have not the knowledge of God: I speak this to your shame.

This is a spiritual wake up call. As we say here in the British Virgin Islands, 'Wake up, (meh son) my son!'

Now a wakeup call is the coming into awareness of something, or the realization of facts that already exist. The Church itself needs a wakeup call to righteousness (which is right living before God) and the entire community needs its own wakeup call to the Church.

Now we have two very important factors here: How can the community wake up to or come into realization of their need to become part of the body of Christ, if the body of Christ is not awake to righteousness, not awake to righteousness of God in Christ Jesus? If indeed the Church is awake to righteousness, then the Body of believers in Christ will not be the partakers and promoters of gossip, lies, adultery, accusations, judging, cheating, backbiting, hatred, jealousy, witchcraft, covetousness and all other things that deny an awareness of righteousness!

God is a Holy God. The disrespect shown for His Word is leaving the Church without a witness of Holiness. This sad circumstance is leaving the community in a state of confusion and despair: if the Christian does not live right, if the Christian does not correct wrongs (in the home, church or the workplace), then the sinner has no example of righteousness to model himself upon!

How, then, can we lead people to a Christian lifestyle that we ourselves are denying by our very actions?

'Awaken to righteousness!' Oh, church of the living God! Awaken to righteousness and sin not! The church has been sleeping while the enemy is leading a double-headed attack! Awaken to righteousness!

When the church of the living God awakens, then the entire community will awaken to righteousness. Do we need hard evidence that we are asleep? Just make a visit to the Magistrate's Court on any given day and see the fruits of sleeping on the job. Young people that have been allowed to have their own way, and lack of moral correction in Christian homes has led to lives stained and messed up by criminal acts. The failure to correct, as the Word of God says to correct, has produced a generation of young people with messed up values and no righteousness to live by.

Awakening to righteousness also means making the hard decisions that will prove beneficial in the long run. Stop being people pleasers! Stop looking for instant love! True love will tell you when you are wrong; true love will correct you when you are wrong no matter how much the heart pains to do it. The instant gratification of people pleasing and in the same action displeasing God has brought us to a frightful position. Awaken to righteousness, so that others may see the righteousness of God and glorify Him.

> *I decide* to take a Holy Spirit-led introspection of myself.
> *I declare* that I will make the unashamed adjustments needed to stand for righteousness and not popularity.
>
> *I recognize* that the future generations need me to stand now, so that they will survive the onslaught of the enemy of their souls.

Are You Abiding?

> **John 15:7**
> *If ye abide in me, and my words abide in you, ye shall ask*
> *what ye will, and it shall be done unto you.*

Before we can answer this question, "Are you abiding?" we must first understand what Jesus means when He speaks about abiding.

Abiding speaks about being *permanent, unshakable* and *steadfast*. Therefore, we must first ponder – not just ask ourselves, but truly contemplate – this point: "Am I permanent, unshakable and steadfast in living according to the Words of Jesus?"

As we ponder, we will all come to areas in which we know (if we are being honest) that we have fallen short. That is not a bad thing! Realization brings us to the point where we need to fix that which is wrong or out of tune. So as we each realize the areas in our lives that need to be fixed or come into tune with the Words of Jesus, we are well on the way to *abiding*.

Now Jesus said *'if you abide in me'*, so that is the first point to ponder: "Am I really in Christ? Have I really had the experience of a changed life in Christ, by way of my personal confession and repentance, and received the Grace of God?" I don't mean just repeating all this in some formal group setting as part of a service program. To put it bluntly, ask, "Am I saved from my sins in which I was born by my personal interaction with the Lord?"

The honesty of the answer opens you the remainder of what Jesus had to say in our scripture – *'ask … and it shall be done unto you'*. For you see, the next step is to have His words abide in you, and you remember what it is to abide – being permanent, unshakable and steadfast in Christ.

Living in this condition will give rise to fulfillment of the promises in our verse, we can ask what we will ... that is pretty broad ... a blank cheque, if you will. That is pretty exciting!

We will have it done unto us ... an assurance of answers to our questions. Isn't that just wonderful? But more than that, it is true! Why then do Christians have all of the struggles that we seem to experience? Maybe it is because we are still learning from our different experiences or maybe we haven't been honest in pondering whether or not we are really abiding. For the Word of God to work in your life, you must fulfill *every* requirement. No partial effort will do.

> *I know that abiding in Him is a choice. I choose to abide in Him, because I know it is the Will of God as my destiny and it is the Father's good pleasure to give me the kingdom.*

> *I declare the peace of abiding, the security of abiding, the comfort of abiding as my portion.*

Blindness

Matthew 20:30-32

30 And, behold, two blind men sitting by the way side, when they heard that Jesus passed by, cried out, saying, Have mercy on us, O Lord, thou son of David.
31 And the multitude rebuked them, because they should hold their peace: but they cried the more, saying, Have mercy on us, O Lord, thou son of David.
32 And Jesus stood still, and called them, and said, What will ye that I shall do unto you?

II Corinthian 4:3-4

3 But if our gospel be hid, it is hid to them that are lost:
4 In whom the god of this world hath blinded the minds of them which believe not, lest the light of the glorious gospel of Christ, who is the image of God, should shine unto them.

There are those who are physically blind, and that is an easy situation to assess. But there are those who are spiritually blind, who are in a very serious circumstance, mostly because they do not realize that they are in a *condition of blindness*. Now, blindness is the inability to see or to perceive what is going on around you.

Blindness to the one struck with that condition is to dwell in darkness. Now, if you close your eyes for a minute, you will see that the darkness which confronts you is not a condition that you will want to exist in for any extended period of time!

These blind men in our scripture wanted desperately to be relieved of their condition, so when the opportunity of hope presented itself, they did the best that they could to seize the opportunity.

Whenever you try to better your condition, you will meet with opposition. The people around them started to rebuke (oppose) them, but they realized and knew that if they listened to those people, they would never get their freedom. I tell you, sometimes you have to ignore the nay-sayers to get to your deliverance, you've got to push past the voices of rejection and discouragement to get your victory. Nothing worth having comes to you without a fight.

I submit to you that these blind men fought very hard to get Jesus' attention, because they realized their condition needed a deliverer and the Great Deliverer was on the scene.

They were convinced that this was their hour of deliverance because they *knew* that they were blind, that is the key: Unlike we who are sighted, *they knew* that they were blind.

An even more serious condition exists in our world today, that is where sighted people are blinded spiritually but do not know it. Oh, this begs for a lot of revelation from the Word of God. You see, if you do not realize and acknowledge your condition, you will never be delivered from it! Subsequently you will be unwilling to take action to correct it.

There are blinded people in the world walking around in a state of spiritual blindness, led by their own convictions of seeing what is right. But they are dead wrong according to the Word of God! These people need to cry out to Jesus for salvation and deliverance. Are you one of them?

> *I pray for the spirit of wisdom and revelation in the knowledge of Christ.*
>
> *I declare spiritual discernment which brings sight to areas of blindness, light to areas of darkness, loosing of fetters, freedom in true knowledge. I will use the Word which is a lamp unto my feet and a light unto my pathway in life.*

Author Bio

Michael U. Anthony holds an associate's degree in digital electronics and robotics from Valencia Community College in Orlando, Florida, and a bachelor's degree in engineering technology from the University of South Florida in Tampa. After graduation, he returned to the British Virgin Islands to work in computer studies and consulting.

Only a few years after moving back to BVI, Anthony received salvation, sanctification, and the baptism of the Holy Ghost, changing the course of his career. Anthony was ordained as a minister in 2000 and currently works in ministry full time with his wife, Monica Frett-Anthony. In addition, Anthony has served on the BVI Teaching Service Commission and chaired both the Board of Immigration and the Road Traffic Advisory Committee.

However, Anthony's true delight is in teaching the tenets of faith to communities in the US and British Virgin Islands and the Eastern Caribbean.

www.ingramcontent.com/pod-product-compliance
Lightning Source LLC
Chambersburg PA
CBHW072015040426
42447CB00009B/1636